D1215311

MATISSE
THE DANCE

MATISSE
THE DANCE

Jack Flam

NATIONAL GALLERY OF ART • WASHINGTON

This book is dedicated to the memory of Pierre Matisse,
who played such an important role in the events it describes, and who
always extended to its author such exemplary goodwill and generosity.

The exhibition of the
Unfinished Dance Mural is made possible by a gift in memory of Pierre Matisse

Copyright © 1993 Board of Trustees, National Gallery of Art, Washington
Text Copyright © 1993 Jack Flam
Copyright © 1993 Succession Henri Matisse, Paris/ARS New York for all
works by Henri Matisse

This book was produced by the editors office, National Gallery of Art.
Editor-in-chief, Frances P. Smyth
Edited by Julie Warnement, with Lys Ann Shore
Designed by Tom Suzuki, with Constance D. Dillman

Library of Congress Cataloging-in-Publication Data

Flam, Jack D.
    Matisse: The Dance/Jack Flam.
        p.   cm.
    ISBN 0–89468–197–4
        1. Matisse, Henri, 1869-1954. Dance. 2. Matisse, Henri, 1869–1954
    — Criticism and interpretation. 3. Mural painting and decoration,
    French— Pennsylvania— Merion. 4. Barnes Foundation.
    I. National Gallery of Art (U.S.)
    ND553, M37A64   1993
    759, 4—dc20   93-15991
                                                            CIP

cover: *Merion Dance Mural* (fig. 2); inside flap of cover: *Unfinished Dance Mural* (fig. 1); frontispiece: Matisse drawing with a bamboo stick (fig. 24); p. 12: *Dancer* (fig. 8)

CONTENTS

5689

The exhibition of two versions of the mural that Matisse painted for the Barnes Foundation and the publication of this book to accompany that exhibition comprise an especially gratifying occasion for the National Gallery of Art. During the past two decades, the National Gallery has mounted three major exhibitions dedicated to various aspects of Matisse's work. In 1977 we inaugurated what is generally regarded as the definitive exhibition of the late cutouts, *Matisse: The Cut-Outs*; in 1986 we organized an equally comprehensive exhibition of the paintings Matisse did during his early Nice period, *Matisse: The Early Years in Nice*; and in 1990 we dedicated a precisely focused show to Matisse's Moroccan works, *Matisse in Morocco*.

Now, within the context of *Great French Paintings from The Barnes Foundation*, we have the privilege of exhibiting for the first time the recently discovered and newly restored *Unfinished Dance Mural*, along with the *Merion Dance Mural*, which was commissioned from the artist by Dr. Barnes in 1930 and installed in Merion exactly sixty years ago, in May 1933. As this book recounts with great insight and sympathy, the Barnes commission came at an especially critical moment in Matisse's career. His work on the mural marked a turning point between his intimate, rather naturalistic paintings of the 1920s and his late decorative style, which culminated in the cutouts. The mural project is thus not only inextricably linked to Matisse's visits to the United States in the early 1930s, but also clearly relates to the themes of two of the National Gallery's previous Matisse shows. For it served as an important point of transition between the early Nice paintings and the late cutouts.

I am enormously grateful to my colleague at the Musée d'art moderne de la Ville de Paris, Suzanne Pagé, for facilitating the loan of the *Unfinished Dance Mural*. Most of all, we are in the debt of the Matisse family—Maria-Gaetana Matisse, Jacqueline Monnier Matisse, Pierre Noël Matisse, Paul Matisse, and Claude Duthuit—for their encouragement of this project.

Jack Flam, one of the world's leading Matisse scholars, gives a compelling and detailed account of the mural project and of its place within Matisse's oeuvre. In his absorbing narrative, Flam vividly evokes both the art-historical and human dimensions of the mural project. This book not only gives a focused and revealing account of a crucial phase in Matisse's career; it also adds a great deal to our knowledge about Matisse himself, and to our appreciation of the immense energy, ingenuity, and courage that he brought to everything he did.

Working closely with Flam at the National Gallery on the exhibition and this publication were Gordon Anson, Susan M. Arensberg, Michelle Fondas, Sally Freitag, Jay Krueger, Mark Leithauser, Ross Merrill, Elizabeth D. Pochter, Gaillard Ravenel, Mervin Richard, Sara Sanders-Buell, Frances Smyth, Jane Sweeney, D. Dodge Thompson, Chris Vogel, and Julie Warnement. ◗

Earl A. Powell III
Director

ACKNOWLEDGMENTS

OST OF THE KEY EVENTS RELATED in this book took place in four cities—New York, Merion, Nice, and Paris—and I want to thank a number of people in those cities for their timely and generous assistance.

In New York, I am profoundly grateful to Maria-Gaetana Matisse and to Paul Matisse for so generously making accessible material from the archives of the Pierre Matisse Foundation and for their enthusiastic and unwavering commitment to this project, from beginning to end. My special thanks also go to Paul Matisse for his invaluable help in organizing the correspondence between Henri Matisse and Pierre Matisse. At the Pierre Matisse Foundation, my thanks also go to Olive Bragazzi and Andrea Farrington for their timely assistance.

In Merion, I owe a special debt of gratitude to Nicolas King of the Barnes Foundation, who has so generously shared with me his extensive knowledge of the foundation archives and who has been so supportive in all phases of this project.

In Nice, I want to thank Xavier Girard of the Musée Matisse for allowing me to examine the studies for the mural while they were in storage and for his timely help with documentation and photographs.

In Paris, I particularly want to thank Claude and Barbara Duthuit for making available to me material from the Matisse Archives, and Wanda de Guébriant for her unflagging patience and resourcefulness in helping me to unravel the complex web of events behind the creation of the various versions of the mural. I am also extremely grateful to Lydia Delectorskaya for sharing with me her memories of her work on the Merion version of the mural and for her valuable insights into Matisse's working methods. My thanks also go to Jacqueline Matisse-Monnier for her enthusiastic support, and to Suzanne Pagé, Juliette Laffon, and Martine Contensou, of the Musée d'art moderne de la Ville de Paris, for their valuable cooperation.

The exhibition of the murals in Washington, D.C., now adds a fifth city to the list. My thanks go to everyone at the National Gallery of Art who has helped with this publication—and most especially to J. Carter Brown, who played such a crucial role in bringing it to fruition. ◼ॱ

A T THE BEGINNING OF 1930 Henri Matisse came to the United States for the first time, and later that year he came back to serve on the jury of the Carnegie International Exhibition. During the second trip, Dr. Albert C. Barnes proposed that Matisse create a mural for the main gallery of the Barnes Foundation in Merion, Pennsylvania. This commission came at a critical time in Matisse's career and precipitated a radical change in his art.

Moreover, a mistake in the measurements was discovered just as Matisse was about to finish the mural. In consequence, he had to start all over again and make a second version, which was eventually installed in Merion. The two versions of the finished mural are usually referred to as *Dance I* and *Dance II,* and they are usually supposed to have followed one another directly. The so-called first version, now in the Musée d'art moderne de la Ville de Paris, is generally thought to have been executed largely in 1931–1932, just before Matisse began the version now in Merion, which was completed in the spring of 1933.

Recently a third, unfinished, full-scale version of the mural was discovered, rolled up and abandoned among unexamined remains from Matisse's last studio in the Hotel Regina, Nice.[1] Examination of this version of the mural has shed new light on the history of the project and on the elaborate technical procedure Matisse invented for it. When I first saw this set of three large canvases in Paris in June 1992, I was struck by the presence of literally hundreds of pinholes all over it. This led me to reconsider just how Matisse had gone about creating the two versions of the finished murals and what the actual sequence of his work on them had been. As I continued my research, I discovered that although the supposed "first version" has "Nice 1932" inscribed at the lower right, it was not finished until late in 1933, well after the Merion mural had been installed. In fact the relationships among the three different full-scale versions of the mural were quite complex and involved considerable overlapping between work on one set of canvases and the other. It became apparent that the different versions should be given descriptive rather than sequential titles. In this essay the recently discovered unfinished painting is referred to as the *Unfinished Dance Mural* (fig. 1), the version in Merion is called the *Merion Dance Mural* (fig. 2), and the version now in the Musée d'art moderne de la Ville de Paris is referred to as the *Paris Dance Mural* (fig. 3).

Intrigued by the complexity of what had at first seemed to be simply

1. *Unfinished Dance Mural*, 1931; pinholes added 1931–1933. Oil on canvas, 341 x 394 cm (*left*), 351 x 498 cm (*center*), 335 x 391 cm (*right*)

Pierre Matisse Estate, Musée d'art moderne de la Ville de Paris purchase/dation

2. *Merion Dance Mural*, 1932–1933. Oil on canvas, 339.7 x 441.3 cm (*left*), 355.9 x 503.2 cm (*center*), 338.8 x 439.4 cm (*right*)

The Barnes Foundation, Merion, Pennsylvania

3. *Paris Dance Mural*, 1931–1933. Oil on canvas, 340 x 387 cm (*left*), 355 x 498 cm (*center*), 335 x 391 cm (*right*)

Musée d'art moderne de la Ville de Paris

an incident in Matisse's life, I turned up a great deal of fresh documentary material pertaining to the whole mural project, including letters, diaries, unpublished photographs of the work in progress, and previously unknown studies for it. This made it possible to unravel the complicated story behind this ambitious undertaking, which marks an important turning point in Matisse's career. Clear parallels also emerged between the *Dance* murals that Matisse executed for the Barnes Foundation and the *Dance* and *Music* panels commissioned by the Russian collector Sergei Shchukin (or Stschoukine) and executed by Matisse in 1909–1910 for Shchukin's home in Moscow.[2] The story told in this essay gives a much more complete view of the Barnes mural project than was previously available and also offers the most detailed study so far of any single phase of Matisse's career. It provides important new information and insights about Matisse the man, as well as about the development of his art. ▪

VOYAGE TO A
NEW WORLD

I N THE LATE 1920S, as Henri Matisse approached his sixtieth birthday, he entered a difficult period in both his life and his art. For the past decade he had been working in an intimate, naturalistic manner very different from the abstract style that had made him a leader of the avant-garde during the years before World War I. But as the decade drew to a close, he began to lose his focus and found it increasingly difficult to paint. At the beginning of this period, he had been extremely prolific; in 1920, for example, he had produced more than sixty paintings. In 1928, however, he painted only about a dozen finished pictures, and in 1929 his production was even smaller.

It is not unusual for an artist to have a painting crisis at this time of life. But in Matisse's case, the change in his artistic life seems to have been closely related to some extreme changes in his domestic situation. In 1920 a young dancer named Henriette Darricarrère had begun modeling for him, and for the next seven years she remained his close companion and principal model. This was the period when Matisse created many of his most sensual paintings, and the attractive young Henriette seems to have been an important source of inspiration for the eroticism of his imagery at this time. Henriette was only nineteen years old when she first met the artist; in 1927, at the age of twenty-six, she left him to establish an independent life and to marry.

The following spring Matisse's wife joined him in Nice, and the tenor of his life changed radically. The couple had not lived together regularly for a decade. This change in personal circumstances directly affected Matisse's art. Shortly after his wife's arrival, he terminated the long series of paintings of odalisques that he had worked on during the past decade and devoted much of his time to graphic works and to sculpture. Working without a model, he began the third head in the *Henriette* series and also worked on *Reclining Nude III*. These sculptures seem to reflect his nostalgia for his departed model, and they also reveal his desire to simplify and condense his vocabulary of forms and to conceive of the surfaces of his sculptures in a less tactile way. Matisse had exhibited at the 1925 Exposition Internationale des Arts Décoratifs et Industriels Modernes, which gave the art deco style its name, and his work toward the end of the decade showed a clear affinity with the streamlined classicism associated with that influential style.

Around the time that Henriette stopped modeling for him, Matisse began to yearn for a change of scene. In 1927 he planned to return to Morocco, where he had traveled in 1912 and 1913 and where his experiences

13

of the place and of the people had had a powerful effect on the development of his painting.[3] But he soon changed his mind and began to plan a trip to Tahiti, where Gauguin had painted and where he could gain a new experience of an exotic and "primitive" place. "One can't live in a house that is too well kept," Matisse told the critic E. Tériade at the beginning of 1929. "One has to go off into the jungle to find simpler ways which won't stifle the spirit."[4]

On the way, Matisse planned to stop in the United States to see museums and private collections and to visit with his son Pierre, who had established himself as an art dealer in New York. Matisse seems to have been rather pressed for cash at this time, and he also hoped to stimulate increased interest in his work among American collectors. Through Pierre, a retrospective exhibition had been organized at the Valentine Gallery in January 1927, and that October Matisse had won the first prize at the Carnegie International Exhibition.

In his 1929 interview with Tériade, Matisse focused on the formal innovations of his fauve paintings and hinted at the changes he desired in his recent work by stating, "Nowadays I seek a certain formal perfection."[5] Later that year, when Matisse was interviewed by Florent Fels, who was writing a monograph on the artist, he said that he was planning a trip to the South Seas, in order "to see the night and dawn light of the Tropics, which doubtless have another density."[6] Typically, Matisse associated his quest for a new inner balance with the experience of new physical sensations: his search for a new inner light was linked to the exploration of a new outer light.

Matisse's restlessness coincided with a period of strong self-doubt. For the first time since the turn of the century, he lacked a clear direction in his art. He had a great deal of trouble starting paintings and even more trouble finishing them. During the winter of 1928 he had hired a new model, Lisette Clarnète, and the next year he had begun a painting of her seated in front of a window wearing an elaborately embellished yellow dress.[7] He was, however, unable to finish this painting until two years later. Other paintings begun around the same time, such as *The Yellow Hat* and *Woman with a Turban,* were never completely resolved.[8]

At this time Matisse was also receiving some adverse criticism, thus compounding his self-doubt with public skepticism about the quality of his work. Even his staunchest supporters were somewhat equivocal about his recent paintings. In a 1929 essay his friend Tériade wrote that "we are far from pretending that Matisse today is working to perfect his canvases.... Thus we will simply say that Matisse is struggling today constantly to maintain the vigor of his legendary flexibility, the youth of his line, the vitality of his color.... He is working to maintain his freedom."[9]

In commemoration of his sixtieth birthday Matisse received a good deal of critical attention. Fels' book was published late in 1929, and during the following year several articles appeared that considered Matisse's stature and historical position. One persistent theme in the writing about him at this time concerns the relative diminution of the quality and ambition of his work during the 1920s. In a review of Matisse's retrospective exhibition at the Thannhauser gallery in February 1930, Fritz Neugass wrote that the artist himself "recognized that he has reached a standstill in his art, for he asks critics to judge him only on the entirety of his works, according to the great curve of his development."[10]

One of the most thoughtful articles to appear at this time was André Levinson's detailed review of Fels' book, which also contained an astute analysis of Matisse's career as a whole—and which seems to anticipate the new direction that Matisse's painting would soon take. Levinson severely criticized Matisse's paintings of the 1920s and took Fels to task for writing a text that emphasized the radicality and originality of Matisse's earlier art while at the same time illustrating the book with so many recent works. "I am quite certain," Levinson wrote, "that the exquisite mannerist of the *Odalisques* would never have been able to turn the art of his age upside down, and to so enrich and guide it."[11] Levinson went on to say that Matisse's great contribution had been in the way he endeavored to apply the principles of decorative painting to easel painting, and in the way he emphasized the surface of the canvas by "inscribing all of the objects in the same plane, bringing them to the surface and reducing them to two dimensions." He praised the bold simplicity of Matisse's earlier paintings, especially his use of pure colors "laid down in broad swaths with uniform intensity, their luminosity unaltered," and the way Matisse was able to simplify his figures and achieve a monumental effect with only three colors in such pictures as the *Dance* and *Music* panels he had painted for Shchukin. If Matisse was a great painter, Levinson concluded, it was because of those early works and not because of his more recent ones.[12]

Matisse's situation was exacerbated by marital problems. Amélie Matisse was chronically bedridden with a spinal disorder, and there was tension between her and Lisette, who had moved in with the Matisses and also served as Amélie's night nurse. It was therefore with some relief that Matisse sailed for New York at the end of February 1930, en route to Tahiti. He arrived in New York on 4 March, and to his pleasant surprise was deeply impressed by the city, which he found so stimulating that he considered terminating his trip there. He reveled in the clarity of the light and the energy of the people, and the day after he arrived he wrote that he felt twenty years younger.[13] "The first time that I saw New York," he stated later, "at seven o'clock in the evening, this gold and black block in the night, reflected in the water, I was in complete ecstasy…. New York seemed to me like a gold nugget."[14]

He remained in New York for a week, engaged in a busy schedule of sightseeing and visiting collectors and collections, before traveling west by train to Chicago, Los Angeles, and San Francisco. From there he went on to Papeete, where he arrived on 29 March, and he spent the next two and a half months in the South Seas. Although Matisse did only one small painting while he was in the Pacific, he spent time traveling around the islands. He was especially impressed by the exotic flora and fauna, and by the coral reefs, which served him as an important source of inspiration in later years. "While swimming underwater with diving glasses on," he wrote to his son Pierre, "I have seen some marvelous landscapes—corals of all colors…and fish of an incredible variety of form and colors—but of a different range from the corals that are higher up, with which they can't be confused, because the color of the lagoon passes from absinthe green to peppermint green and to a blue such as I have never seen except in the Blue Grotto in Capri."[15]

When Matisse returned to France, however, he said that in Tahiti he had had "no pictorial reaction whatsoever," and that his chief feeling there was of a lassitude that was "stronger than everything else."[16] Although in his late cutouts he repeatedly made use of his experiences in the South Seas, in 1930 his style of painting could not easily accommodate the extravagant exoticism that he encountered there. Only when he stopped working directly from nature was he able to use his memories of Oceania in a vivid and meaningful way.

Instead Matisse first used Polynesian themes in sculpture, where he was already accustomed to working from memory. Shortly after he returned to Nice, he began two sculptures directly related to his experiences in the Pacific: *Tiari*, which is based upon a tropical plant, and *Venus on a Shell*, a concentrated evocation of the lush sensuality of the tropics. His experiences in the South Seas were also reflected in the tropical imagery of some of the etchings he made for *Poésies* by Stéphane Mallarmé, a book he had agreed to illustrate for the Swiss publisher Albert Skira shortly before he left France.[17]

On his return to Nice he also reworked *The Yellow Dress,* but was still unable to bring it to a satisfactory conclusion.[18]

ONLY A FEW MONTHS LATER, Matisse took advantage of an opportunity to return to the United States. As a former Carnegie prize winner, he was invited to spend two weeks in the United States as a member of the 1930 Carnegie International Exhibition jury, along with Bernard Karfiol, Karl Sterrer, and Glyn Philpot.[19] He accepted the invitation and returned to New York on the *Mauretania,* which arrived around midnight on 19 September. Matisse disembarked the next morning, in the company of Homer Saint-Gaudens, the director of the Carnegie Institute. The same day he cabled Dr. Barnes about visiting the Barnes Foundation: "Would greatly appreciate being able to visit Barnes Foundation and meet you." Barnes responded immediately: "Delighted to have you come Saturday or Sunday of next week."[20]

At this time the Barnes Foundation had the largest private collection of Matisse paintings in the world, including some of his early masterworks, such as *Le bonheur de vivre* (fig. 4).[21] Matisse was no doubt eager to see such a large and important body of his own work and also to meet the man who had put it together. Barnes, for his part, esteemed Matisse most highly among all living artists and was already planning to write a book about him. Constantly at war with museum curators and art historians, Barnes must also have felt that getting to know the artist personally would give him added authority in his frequent disagreements with those who opposed him.

Saint-Gaudens had arranged for the jury members to be given a brief tour of Washington and Philadelphia after they finished their duties in Pittsburgh (where they awarded first prize to Picasso's 1923 *Portrait of Madame Picasso*). An appointment was made with Barnes for the morning of Saturday, 27 September, while the group would be in Philadelphia on the way back from Washington. Matisse was to be taken to Merion that morning, accompanied by John F. L. Raschen, professor of modern languages at the University of Pittsburgh, who was serving as the group's translator. Barnes was very particular about who set foot in his foundation, and the other members of the jury were not invited along with Matisse; they went instead to the Philadelphia Museum of Art. Nor was Barnes—who was

4. *Le bonheur de vivre,* 1905–1906. Oil on canvas, 174 x 238.1 cm

The Barnes Foundation, Merion, Pennsylvania

usually at odds with most of Philadelphia society—invited to any of the events planned for the group that day. These included a luncheon at the Merion home of Mrs. John Braun, wife of the president of the Philadelphia Art Alliance, and a visit to the Widener collection at Elkins Park.

When Barnes met Matisse and Raschen at the door of the foundation at ten o'clock that morning, he unceremoniously informed the professor that the services of a translator would not be needed and instructed him to come back for Matisse at noon. Alone with the artist, Barnes showed him his collection, which was especially strong in the works of Cézanne and Renoir, the modern artists that Matisse most admired, as well as in his own works. The two men discussed art and how it could best be taught and displayed. Much to Matisse's surprise, Barnes also informed him that he had been waiting enthusiastically for his visit because he wanted him to paint a mural for the lunettes over the large french windows in the foundation's main gallery.

The building had been completed only a few years earlier, in 1925. It was designed by the French-born architect Paul Philippe Cret in a modernized French renaissance style that had many points in common with art deco architecture. It is an austere, well-proportioned building, constructed of handsome buff-colored French limestone, and Matisse seems to have been favorably impressed by both the building and the installation of the paintings within it.

The irregularly shaped area that Barnes had designated for the murals, however, was a difficult space. The three lunettes were created by small lateral transverse vaults that intersected with the barrel vault of the ceiling, creating the effect of pointed arches. The lunettes were separated by the rather wide pendentives of the arches, and because the gallery was high and narrow, a mural would not be easily seen from the floor below. A better view would be offered from an arcaded first-floor balcony, or loggia, directly opposite the lunettes, but here too the view would not be entirely unimpeded. Moreover, because the mural area was set above three glass-paned doors, the painting would be seen against the daylight that came through the glass. The difficulties inherent in composing a mural for such a space were obvious—and further compounded by the presence of many large masterpieces on the other walls of the gallery. Indeed, Matisse later characterized the space as "not being very favorable" for such a painting.[22] But he was intrigued by the challenge that the project offered. Creating such a mural would take him far away from easel painting and force him to work in a truly architectural manner—in a style quite different from the *intimiste* kind of painting he had been involved with for the past ten years.

Matisse hesitated. He was already committed to one long-term project, the book for Skira, and he told Barnes that he would need some time to think about the proposition. In the meantime, the two men had completely forgotten about poor Raschen, who had been desperately ringing the door-bell with no response. Determined at all costs to get Matisse to the luncheon on time, Raschen finally climbed down a coal chute, made his way into the gallery where Barnes and Matisse were talking, and spirited the artist away.[23]

It is generally thought that Barnes' ignoring the doorbell was simply another instance of his legendary disdain for social convention. But it is very likely that he and Matisse were so absorbed in conversation that neither of them heard it—or, in any case, wanted to hear it. Matisse, who generally disliked social events, had been caught up in an extremely busy schedule for the past week, and Barnes' seriousness and intensity of purpose created an appealing island of sanity within the maelstrom of social events. In Barnes he found a man not unlike himself, one who had little patience for social niceties and polite chatter and who was passionately involved with matters of art and philosophy. Barnes had had the means to acquire a superb collection of paintings; he also had the sensibility to exhibit it in a way that Matisse considered appealing and challenging— very different from the theatrical way in which he felt most American museums and collectors showed their art. In his pocket diary for the day of his visit with Barnes, he noted, "the only sane place"—in marked contrast to his scribbled remark about the Widener collection, which he saw later that same day: "the tomb of masterpieces."[24]

Intrigued by Barnes and his collection, as well as by the offer of the commission, Matisse delayed his scheduled departure for France and returned to Merion on 1 October to discuss the matter further.[25] When he left New York two days later, the commission was evidently very much on his mind. The day after he returned to Paris he wrote to Barnes, apparently to express his continued interest in the mural project and to firm up plans for the two men to meet in France.[26]

The prospect of the mural commission seems to have energized Matisse. During the next few weeks, he worked on the fourth and final version of his large bas-relief, *Back IV* (fig. 5), in which he tried out in sculpture the same sort of monumental simplification of the human body that he later used in the mural.[27] He also gave a series of interviews to Tériade, in which he discussed his recent travels and described his reactions to the Barnes Foundation, which had had a marked effect on his thoughts about the future of American art. "One of the most striking things in America is the Barnes collection," he told Tériade, "which is exhibited in a spirit very beneficial for the training of American artists…. This collection presents the paintings in complete frankness, which is not frequent in America. The Barnes Foundation will doubtless manage to destroy the artificial and disreputable presentation of the other collections, where the pictures are hard to see—displayed hypocritically in the mysterious light of a temple or cathedral. According to the current American aesthetic, this presentation seeks to introduce a certain supposedly favorable mystery between the spectator and the work, but it is in the end only a great misunderstanding."[28]

In this interview, Matisse also discussed how his voyages had affected

his frame of mind. "When you have worked for a long time in the same milieu," he remarked, "it is useful at a given moment to stop the usual mental routine and take a voyage which will let parts of the mind rest while other parts have free rein—especially those parts repressed by the will. This stopping permits a withdrawal and consequently an examination of the past. You begin again with more certainty when the preoccupation of the first part of the trip, not having been destroyed by the numerous impressions of the new world you are plunged into, takes possession of the mind again."[29] Matisse also referred to a theme that seems to have been brought to his attention by his visit to the Barnes Foundation: "that the artist can attain his complete development only on the soil where he is born." He repeated this theme to American artists and mentioned it in a cover story in the 20 October 1930 issue of *Time* magazine, where he was quoted as saying, "American artists should not be ashamed of their country, it is magnificent." He was said to have added, "Why do so many American painters continually go abroad when they have at home scenes of such varied beauty?"[30] But on this second point, there is some question as to whether he was accurately quoted. He later asserted that he did not say American artists should avoid traveling abroad to study, but rather that after their studies abroad they should return to their native soil.[31] In suggesting such a program, he seems to have been directly reflecting his recent conversations with Barnes.

BARNES CAME TO PARIS TOWARD THE END of the month and met with Matisse to discuss the details of the mural commission, mostly likely including the price.[32] A few weeks later Matisse returned to the United States, for the third time that year, in order to study the space and work out other details related to the commission. He was met at the pier by Barnes' friend, the philosopher John Dewey, who sat for several portrait drawings at this time. They arrived in Merion at six o'clock that same evening, and Matisse spent the next day studying the space for the mural and observing the activities of the foundation. On 17 and 18 December he was in Baltimore to see Etta Cone, who for some years had been one of his most important collectors. She and her recently deceased sister, Claribel Cone, had collected Matisse's work since 1906, and by 1930 their collection of Matisses included about twenty-five oil paintings, eleven sculptures, and several prints and drawings.[33] Miss Cone was still actively collecting Matisse at the time, and her collection of his work was the only one in the United States that seriously rivaled that of Barnes.

Matisse returned to Merion on 19 December, and the next day Barnes gave him a letter of agreement for the mural, along with a cheque for $10,000. The written agreement called for a second payment of $10,000 "when the work is half done," with a third payment due when the paintings were installed at the foundation. It was further stated that "the work will take about one (1) year to finish."[34] This was a substantial amount of money, and Matisse was apparently quite pleased with the arrangements he had made. Later, however, he came to believe that Barnes had gotten the better part of the bargain.

While Matisse was in Merion, he did some compositional sketches for the mural. "Everything is going well," he wrote to his wife on 22 December. "I have already done a drawn sketch in front of the surface to be decorated. I am full of strength and enthusiasm."[35] He and Barnes continued to get along quite well. Both men were energetic and strong-willed, and they had a deep, if somewhat cautious, respect for each other.[36] They engaged in intense conversations about the creation and interpretation of works of art, and shortly after Matisse's visit, Barnes expressed his enormous enthusiasm about the artist to Dewey: "It was a great experience with him. He is there all the way and back."[37]

Matisse was equally enthusiastic about Barnes, who he realized had an intensity and focus similar to his own, though expressed in a rougher way. "Barnes is very nice," he wrote to his wife. "We have several points in common, but I am less brutal."[38] Barnes must also have reminded Matisse a bit of Sergei Shchukin, another thoughtful and rather eccentric foreign patron, who had been one of his greatest admirers, had amassed a large collection of his paintings, and in the years before the Russian Revolution had had unfailing faith in him and his work.[39]

Barnes was very pleased with Matisse's first sketches, and while the artist was still in Merion a template was made directly from the wall where the mural would be placed, in order to guide the construction of the canvases on which the paintings would be executed.[40] At this time Matisse had little idea of the magnitude of the undertaking, and he anticipated that he would have a relatively easy time with the project. "I am full of hope and zeal," he wrote his wife, "because I have done a sketch in front of the panel [area]. I have seen the plan of the figures on the panel itself and I have decided on the colors. I think that this will not be difficult for me because I feel that my year of rest has resulted in great progress in terms of clarity of mind."[41]

The mural project turned out to be infinitely more difficult than the artist had anticipated. But his new energy and clarity of mind did enable him at last to finish *The Yellow Dress* shortly after he returned to Nice and to prepare himself to work on the largest painting he had ever undertaken.[42] ▪

A NEW
TECHNIQUE

IN ORDER TO HAVE ADEQUATE SPACE to work on such a large project, Matisse rented a vacant garage at 8, rue Désiré-Niel in Nice.[43] He was scrupulous about trying to duplicate the proper ambience for the murals, as can be seen in a description of his setup written by Edward Dreibelbies, a teacher at the Barnes Foundation, who visited Matisse in August 1931: "His procedure is thorough—he explains that the garage is of about the length and width of the large gallery [of the Barnes Foundation], the point of view is that from the balcony. Repainted walls duplicate the plaster and a new sky-light duplicates the illumination. He speaks vividly of the position of other paintings in the room, the Indian blankets, and the landscape which will appear thru the windows. He is enthusiastic and says he is pleased with progress so far."[44]

At the time Matisse was given the commission by Barnes, he was also given free choice of subject, and it was he who decided on the theme of the dance. Barnes, according to the artist, told him that he should execute the work in complete freedom, "as if doing it for yourself."[45] Dance had been the theme of Matisse's first major mural commission, for the Moscow home of Sergei Shchukin in 1909–1910, and Matisse had originally depicted it in *Le bonheur de vivre* (fig. 4), which Barnes had already owned for nearly a decade.

Matisse's choice of this theme at this particular time in his career is significant. For the past several years he had been painting mostly intimate interiors depicted in terms of a rather specific light and ambience, in a naturalistic manner that stood in marked contrast to the more abstract styles of his earlier work. The dance was a conceptual theme that he would have to deal with in a pictorially abstracted, universalized way. Returning to the theme of the dance was a way of returning to his artistic roots, which were superbly represented at the Barnes Foundation. And given the Mallarméan overtones of *Le bonheur de vivre,* it is also significant that Matisse undertook the Barnes commission while working on his illustrations for *Poésies* by Stéphane Mallarmé, which employ imagery clearly related to that of the murals.[46]

Matisse associated the theme of the dance with vitality and rejuvenation. "Dance is an extraordinary thing—life and rhythm," he later said, and throughout his life he associated the dance with a kind of primitive potency.[47] According to the artist, the round of dancers in *Le bonheur de vivre* had been inspired by his encounter with Catalan fishermen dancing a sardana on the beach at Collioure in the summer of 1905. In 1909 he had adapted the round of six dancers from that painting for the panel with five dancers commissioned by Sergei Shchukin (figs. 6–7).

At the time he was working on the Shchukin painting, Matisse was fond of going to the Moulin de la Galette on Sundays to watch people dance, especially the farandole; and he later said that he sang the same tune he had heard at the Moulin de la Galette while he was working on the painting.[48] The subject of the Shchukin panel thus combined two different kinds of direct experiences with popular dancing: the grave and stately Catalan folk dance, and a Parisian version of the livelier Provençal farandole. At the time that Matisse began the panel for Shchukin, he was also fascinated by the energetic performances of the Ballets Russes, which made its Parisian debut

6. *Dance I,* 1909. Oil on canvas, 259.7 x 390.1 cm

The Museum of Modern Art, New York, Gift of Nelson A. Rockefeller in honor of Alfred H. Barr, Jr.

7. *Dance II,* 1909–1910. Oil on canvas, 260 x 391 cm

The Hermitage Museum, St. Petersburg

in May 1909. The Ballets Russes may well have inspired him to treat the second version of the Shchukin commission with greater vigor and physicality, in contrast to the trancelike serenity of the version now in New York.

During the first decade of the century, the dance theme had been closely associated with other intellectual and social concerns. The influence of Nietzsche was especially strong, in particular his notion of the dance as a vivid, liberating embodiment of the Dionysian principle. This is articulated in a famous passage from *The Birth of Tragedy,* with which Matisse was certainly familiar: "In song and in dance man expresses himself as a member of a higher community; he has forgotten how to walk and speak, he is about to take a dancing flight into the air…. He feels himself a god, he himself now walks about enchanted, in ecstasy, like to the gods whom he saw walking about in his dreams."[49] Dance was also linked to physical, social, and moral well-being. Dancing was associated with sport and physical discipline, and was even held up as an activity that would benefit the French public in its political and economic competition with Germany.[50]

It is also significant that two of Matisse's principal models during the 1920s, Henriette and Lisette, had been trained as dancers. Matisse had designed the decor for Diaghilev's 1920 production of *Le chant du rossignol,* and as recently as 1928 the Russian impresario had proposed that Matisse execute designs for another ballet; although the project never materialized, Matisse made several drawings and prints of dancers around that time.[51] In fact, he seems to have had actual dance movements very much in mind when he began to work out his ideas for the Barnes mural. While in Merion the previous December, he had written to his wife asking her to tell his model Lisette "to do what is necessary to be in top physical form, because I am going to have need of her."[52] Lisette herself later recalled that at the same time that she was working on the mural as Matisse's studio assistant, she also posed for studies for the figures (figs. 8, 56): "After having posed nude, I put on my blouse and climbed up the enormous rolling platform to pin the drawing to the wall."[53]

The dance also provided Matisse with a subject for a public place that was relatively contemplative and private. In contrast to the contemporary Mexican muralists, such as Diego Rivera, Matisse was not interested in an art that addressed broad social issues; nor was Barnes, who ran his foundation as a private fiefdom despite its legal status as a public institution. In May 1933, when Matisse was asked about Rivera's controversial mural at Rockefeller Center in New York City, he responded: "Politics are temporary, they pass. Art lives on forever. I do not believe in propaganda art. It is not necessary for the artist to associate himself with the class struggle or for him to seek to interpret it."[54] And indeed the year before, when Matisse had been asked to submit a design for the entrance hall of the RCA building at Rockefeller Center, he had declined to do so. The proposed theme was "New Frontiers—The March of Civilization," and Matisse made it clear, as Alfred Barr has noted, that "he did not think his work could be

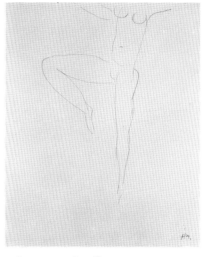

8. *Dancer,* 1931. Pencil on paper, 30.1 x 25.7 cm
Musée Matisse, Nice

seen to good advantage in such a public place where bustle and confusion would interfere with the quiet, reflective state of mind which he felt necessary for the appreciation of his paintings."[55] Matisse's only previous commission for large decorative paintings, the *Dance* and *Music* panels that he had done for Sergei Shchukin in 1909–1910, had also been painted with the public space of a private house in mind.

Matisse used the Shchukin *Dance* (see figs. 6–7) as his point of departure for the composition as well as the subject of the Barnes mural, which was his first painting of figures in motion since he had finished the 1910 *Dance*. When he began work on the first small studies for the mural, he pinned to a nearby wall reproductions of his 1909 full-size oil sketch for the *Dance* and of a charcoal drawing he had done for the 1910 version (see fig. 9). In some of the earliest small drawings he made for the Barnes *Dance,* the composition follows the 1909–1910 composition quite closely, with the pendentives of the architecture functioning merely as "interruptions" of the round of dancers rather than as a structural component (fig. 10).

Matisse may have made some of these small drawings, which are on pocket drawing-pad paper, in Merion (fig. 11). Others were done shortly

9. Matisse working on sketches for the Barnes mural, 1931

10. *Study for Barnes Mural Composition,* 1931.
Pencil on paper, 27.7 x 37.7 cm

Musée Matisse, Nice

11. *Study for Barnes Mural,* 1930. Pencil
on paper, 26 x 33.1 cm

Musée Matisse, Nice

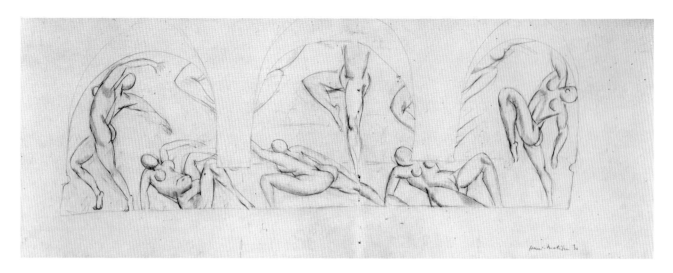

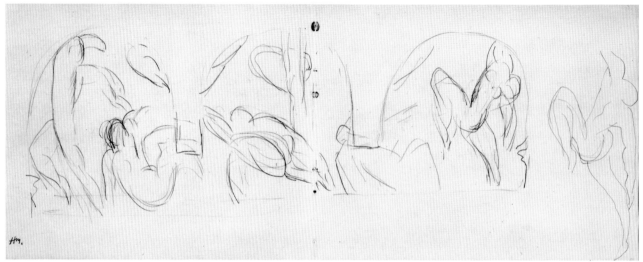

12. *Study for Barnes Mural Composition,*
(1930?) 1931. Pencil on paper, 28.2 x 76.2 cm

Musée Matisse, Nice

13. *Study for Barnes Mural Composition,* 1931.
Pencil on paper, 25.5 x 66.3 cm

Musée Matisse, Nice

14. *Study for Barnes Mural Composition,* 1931.
Pencil on paper, 25.4 x 66.2 cm

Musée Matisse, Nice

15. *Study for Barnes Mural Composition*, 1931.
Pencil on tracing paper, 49.5 x 65 cm
Private collection

after he returned to Nice. These reveal his search for the general outlines of the composition and also for a suitable manner of rendering. They range from tightly rendered, carefully modeled figures (fig. 12), to rather sketchy and electric evocations of a more ethereal sort of dance (figs. 13–14). Matisse made tracings of some of these small studies and apparently gave them to Barnes as a kind of record of progress. At least one of the drawings may have been rendered from a photograph of the wall in the Barnes Foundation (fig. 15). Matisse had sent photographs of the foundation building back to his wife in Nice at the end of December 1930, and some of the compositions on tracing paper may have been done with the paper laid over photographs of the wall.[56]

The differences in the widths of the pendentives in these early compositional studies are especially interesting, since it was the miscalculation of those widths that led Matisse to execute the first version of the mural on canvases that were the wrong shape and size. In the earlier studies, including those that appear to have been done in Merion, Matisse seems to have gotten the widths of the pendentives nearly right, since he was working directly from the architectural surface (figs. 16–17). But even here he was

16. *Study for Barnes Mural Composition,* 1931.
Pencil on paper, 25.8 x 33.2 cm
Musée Matisse, Nice

17. *Study for Barnes Mural Composition,* 1931.
Pencil on paper, 25.6 x 66.4 cm
Musée Matisse, Nice

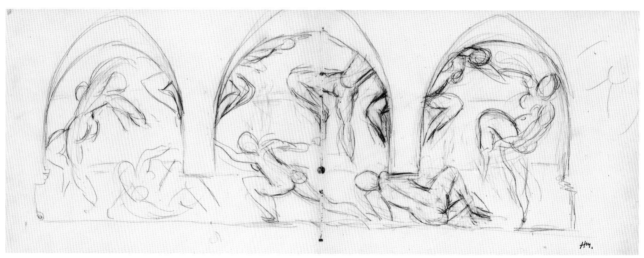

only "nearly" right, because we already see a tendency on his part to make the pendentives a little narrower than they really were, in order to harmonize better with his compositional ideas. In effect, he was unconsciously altering the architecture so that it would better accommodate his conception of the mural.[57] As the work progressed, he also made drawings that incorporated studies of the background planes (fig. 18) and at least one full-size drawing in order to fully grasp the actual scale (fig. 19).

Virtually all the early studies are based directly on the Shchukin *Dance* composition. Like the 1909–1910 painting, many of them have explicit landscape elements, such as a ground line or a horizon line; some even have foliage drawn in the landscape (figs. 10, 12). The poses of the figures in the small oil studies (figs. 20–22), like those in the drawings on which they are

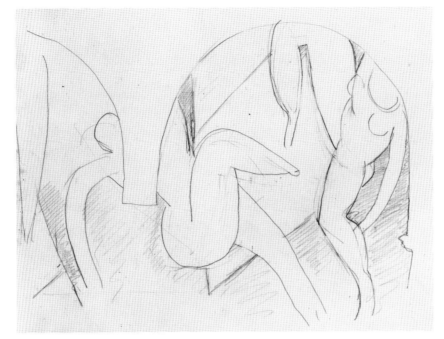

18. *Study for Center and Right Panels of Barnes Mural Composition,* 1931. Pencil on paper, 23.9 x 32 cm
Musée Matisse, Nice

based, are also derived from those in the 1909 painting—although with modifications that take into account the irregular shapes and architectural context of the Barnes commission. The rendering in these early oil sketches involves a certain amount of modeling, and the poses and facture recall the figures in Cézanne's *Three Bathers,* which Matisse himself owned (fig. 23). The background is still conceived as a simplified landscape, and the composition is rather stiff.

19. *Drawing for Center Figure of Barnes Mural,* 1931. Brush and ink on paper, 335 x 198 cm
Musée Matisse, Nice

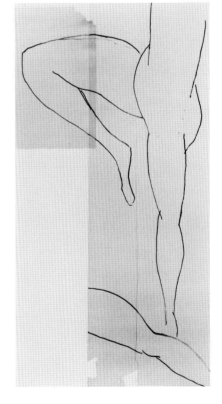

BY EARLY APRIL 1931 Matisse had set up the large canvases on which he planned to execute the actual pictures, having decided to work out the final composition at full scale rather than from small sketches that would eventually be squared up.[58] In a draft of a letter to Barnes, which was apparently never sent, Matisse wrote that he had just finished installing the large canvases for the murals in his studio. He described what he called the "superhuman" dimensions of the canvases and said that he had begun drawing directly on them but was still uncertain about the colors he would employ. He also remarked ironically that although he had grasped the canvases in spirit, his body had not grown accordingly and that he had had to find another means of extending his arms and legs—apparently through the use of the bamboo stick that he can be seen employing in a photograph taken at the time (fig. 24).[59]

Here, as in all the later versions of the mural, Matisse worked on a set of three rectangular canvases on which he inscribed the rounded arches of the spaces to be painted, surmounted by pointed arches to remind him of the pictorial dynamics of the architecture. When the pictures were finished, the excess canvas could be folded back and attached to stretchers built in the shape of the lunettes that they were intended to fill. Initially,

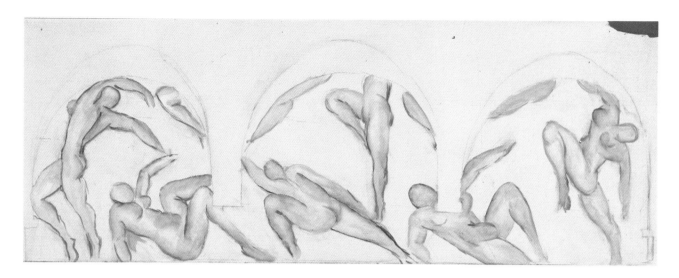

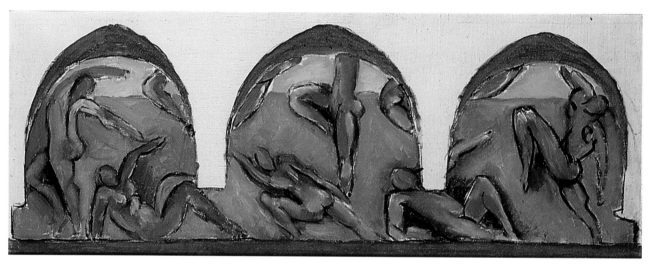

20. *Oil Study for Barnes Mural, Gray Harmony,* 1931. Oil on canvas, 32 x 86.5 cm
Musée Matisse, Nice

21. *Oil Study for Barnes Mural, Ocher Harmony,* 1931. Oil on canvas, 32 x 86.5 cm
Musée Matisse, Nice

22. *Oil Study for Barnes Mural, Blue Harmony,* 1931. Oil on canvas, 32 x 86.5 cm
Musée Matisse, Nice

Matisse had also planned to paint decorative panels in the irregularly shaped areas around the composition proper, in a manner reminiscent of Italian renaissance fresco decoration, but he later abandoned this notion.[60] Traces of this project are still visible within the borders of the *Unfinished Dance Mural*, the first full-scale attempt at painting the mural, which was begun on the canvas that was later abandoned and only recently rediscovered (fig. 1).

Although it is not known whether or not Matisse made a cartoon to help transfer the small sketches to the large canvases, it is quite possible that he did, at least to set the main lines of the composition (which could later be drawn over or modified, as we see in the photograph of him working on the large canvases). He had probably used a cartoon for the second version of the 1909–1910 *Dance,* and the composition of the *Unfinished Dance Mural* is close enough to some of the early sketches to suggest that if he did not actually make a detailed cartoon, he nonetheless followed the small compositional drawings quite closely when he made the transition to the large canvases.[61]

On 24 April Matisse gave Barnes a progress report and sent two series of photographs of what he had done so far—which he characterized as "first contact with the surface," and "second attack, more architectural, I believe"—and said that "at present, I am searching for the colors."[62] These photographs are of the first charcoal drawings that Matisse did directly on the canvas and are inscribed in Matisse's hand, "1er dessin sur toile" and "2e dessin sur la toile." While the first drawing (visible in fig. 24) follows some of the small sketches quite closely, in the second (fig. 25) Matisse has already begun to think in terms of making the figures fill more of the picture space.[63] That Matisse continued to make small studies even after he had begun to draw on the large canvases is clear from a draft of this letter that he sent to his daughter Marguerite on 10 April: "At this moment, I am working on the small sketches and making small studies in order to help me in the execution."[64] It seems fairly certain from this letter that the small oil sketches (figs. 20–22) were made after Matisse had begun to draw on the large canvases, in order to concentrate on the problems of color and facture. The project of adding color, intriguingly arrested at an early stage in the *Unfinished Dance Mural,* was undertaken only after Matisse had studied a number of different options.

Barnes wrote to Matisse on 5 May, expressing his satisfaction with the photographs that Matisse had sent, but saying he was disturbed by the fact that the canvas did not seem to be large enough to allow for borders that could be folded back over the stretchers. "According to the photos," Barnes said, "it seems that the canvas containing the figures is joined to the piece representing the sky without any border to allow for mounting the canvas with the figures on the stretcher. Now, our intention being to place them on the stretchers by folding back the excess, it is necessary to leave a rather large border all around the painting, a border of at least three or four

23. Paul Cézanne, *Three Bathers,* c. 1879–1882. Oil on canvas, 60.3 x 54.6 cm
Musée du Petit Palais, Paris

centimeters, which would be folded back around the stretchers."[65] In the same letter Barnes told Matisse that the wood for the stretchers had already been ordered so that it would be properly cured to provide as stable a support as possible.

On 15 May Matisse replied to Barnes "to reassure you immediately." He explained that there would be no problem about having large enough borders to stretch the pictures and included a drawing (fig. 26) to explain which parts of the canvas he had left in reserve to be folded back around the mural (marked *a* in the drawing) and which parts would be painted around the mural proper (marked *b* on the drawing). The pointed arches that Barnes had interpreted as sky, he pointed out, were "only done to help me in the composition—it is a fragment of canvas that will not be included on your wall."[66]

Although he had seen only photographs and sketches of the mural, Barnes was confident enough about its progress to make the second $10,000 payment to Matisse on 16 June 1931, while he was in Paris to see the large Matisse retrospective at the Galeries Georges Petit.[67] At this time Barnes was in high spirits, actively buying Matisse paintings and hard at work on his book about the artist, which he was writing in collaboration with Violette de Mazia. While in Paris he composed a thousand pages of analytic notes in front of Matisse's paintings.[68] It is said that when Barnes met Matisse there, he only half jokingly asked him why he wasn't back in Nice working on the mural.[69]

24. Matisse drawing with a bamboo stick, 1931

The Barnes Foundation, Merion, Pennsylvania

Barnes remained skeptical about the adequacy of the canvas borders, so he sent Dreibelbies to Nice that summer to confirm that there would indeed be enough canvas to fold back behind the stretchers. The amount of canvas was perfectly adequate, given the dimensions that Matisse was working with, but this issue drew attention away from the larger issue of whether those dimensions were themselves correct. When Dreibelbies wrote to Barnes on 2 August, he included a detailed drawing of Matisse's layout for the canvases, complete with dimensions (fig. 27).

"The mural as laid out by Matisse is on three rectangular canvases," he explained to Barnes, indicating their general shape with dotted lines on his drawing. He continued, "Matisse says the architectural measurements are exact—the figures given locate the divisions [between the three separate canvases]." Dreibelbies also assured Barnes that "a generous width of canvas has been allowed on all four sides and Matisse is painting about two inches of canvas on 'turned in' edges where the two divisions occur.

"Matisse was interested in checking the measurements as they were taken and wishes to say that two or three months prior to the completion of the painting he will send complete and detailed information—also, he

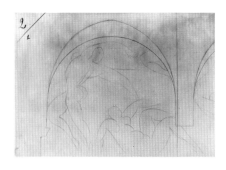

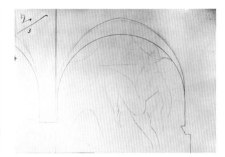

25. Photographs of second compositional drawings on canvases of Barnes mural, April 1931

The Barnes Foundation, Merion, Pennsylvania

26. Drawing in a letter from Matisse to Barnes, 15 May 1931

The Barnes Foundation, Merion, Pennsylvania

intends to inquire as to the practicability of an aluminum chassis for lightness, rigidity, and permanence."[70]

The matter of the dimensions was apparently settled—even though the diagram in Dreibelbies' letter indicates the width of the pendentive bases as being around 21 inches (about 53 cm) each. This figure is clearly wrong,

since the pendentive bases in the building are actually about 1 meter wide—
nearly twice as wide as those indicated in the diagram. As far as we know,
Barnes did not notice this discrepancy at the time. This lends credence to
the assertion that "Barnes had never learned to read a blueprint," and that
it was his wife who had served as his liaison with the architect and builders
while the foundation building was under construction.[71]

In the early oil sketches Matisse had experimented with predominantly
ocher and blue color harmonies. For the first experiment with color on the
full-scale mural, he also kept his colors reduced, this time to blue and gray.
The *Unfinished Dance Mural* follows quite closely the composition of some
of the small sketches (see figs. 12, 17). The drawing and the brushwork in it
are remarkably fresh, and its surface is very matte and frescolike. Its marked
resemblance to early renaissance fresco underpaintings indicates that from
the beginning Matisse sought a paint surface that would harmonize with
the architecture. But the rendering of the figures in this version is still

27. Diagram in letter from Dreibelbies
to Barnes, 2 August 1931

The Barnes Foundation, Merion,
Pennsylvania

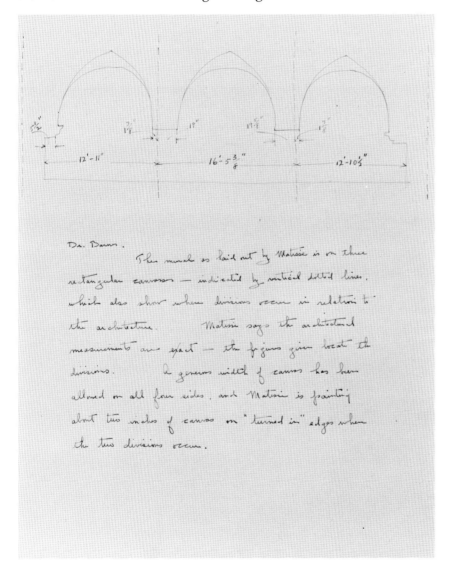

much more pictorial than architectural: the view of the dancers in space takes precedence over the architectural surface design. In essence there are two systems in conflict here, the one pictorial, descriptive, and painterly, the other flat, decorative, and architectural.

This conflict proved to be an insurmountable problem, since the constant play of the brush was at odds with the architectural effect that Matisse was seeking. Moreover, this early version of the mural retains a strong sense of an implied landscape background that is related to the 1909–1910 *Dance,* and this too was incompatible with the architectural setting.

Matisse was in a quandary, and at this point he turned to an unexpected source for inspiration. About a month after Dreibelbies' visit, Matisse went to Italy to rest at Abano Bagno and to see Giotto's frescoes in the Arena Chapel at Padua. Since his first visit to Padua in 1907, Matisse had associated Giotto with the highest ambitions of monumental art. He later referred to Giotto as "the summit of my desires."[72] And now, at a moment of doubt, he turned for inspiration to the Italian master, one of the greatest of all mural painters.[73] When he returned to Nice, he seems to have already decided that he would have to take his mural in a radically different direction. At this point he abandoned work on what is now the *Unfinished Dance Mural* and began to work on top of it, on the same three canvases, with pieces of cut and pinned paper (figs. 28–30). This new technique more or less forced him to reduce his range of colors and to suppress modeling and the illusion of deep space.[74]

The use of cut paper helped Matisse create the kind of architectural effect that he was seeking in a way that he could not achieve with his usual painting technique, which employed subtly nuanced brushwork and in which the figures were conceived as moving within an illusionistically conceived space. His new technique also served a practical function, for Matisse had found that the enormous scale of the mural required frequent and extensive changes that would be very difficult to achieve by constant repainting. The cut-paper technique offered a convenient and ingenious way of trying out compositional changes without having to do extensive repainting. The sheets of paper pinned to the surface of the canvas could be easily altered by moving them around and by cutting them. Matisse could thus make changes in the composition without having to rub out, paint over, or build up a thick surface filled with pentimenti.

The method that Matisse developed was as follows: He engaged a housepainter named Goyo to paint large sheets of paper in the limited number of colors that he had decided on for the composition: gray for the figures, and blue, pink, and black for the background. These sheets of paper were stacked in piles, to be used like a palette. As these sheets of paper were employed, they could be cut to conform to the shapes that Matisse wanted and secured to the surface of the canvas with pins. Matisse would modify the shapes on the canvas by drawing over them with charcoal; his assistant would then trim the edges with scissors to conform to

28. Photograph of beginning of the cut-paper composition for *Paris Dance Mural,* 1931

The Barnes Foundation, Merion, Pennsylvania

29. Photograph of *Paris Dance Mural* in progress, 1931

The Barnes Foundation, Merion, Pennsylvania

30. Photograph of *Paris Dance Mural* in progress, 1931

The Barnes Foundation, Merion, Pennsylvania

MATISSE: THE DANCE

the new contours. Eventually, when the composition was fixed, the plan was to lift the areas of cut paper and fill in the canvas below with the same color oil paint that had been used on the sheets of paper.[75] In fact, the first coats of paint would be applied to the canvases by the same housepainter, in order to ensure a wall-like flatness and impersonality of surface.

This was a radical departure from Matisse's previous technique. It permitted him to make large changes quickly, and it also depersonalized his relationship to the surface of the picture, in accordance with his notion of creating an "architectural" rather than an "expressive" surface. He emphasized the architectural function of the mural by flattening the space and by increasing the size of the figures in relation to the total image, so as to give the panels the commanding presence that their architectural setting required.

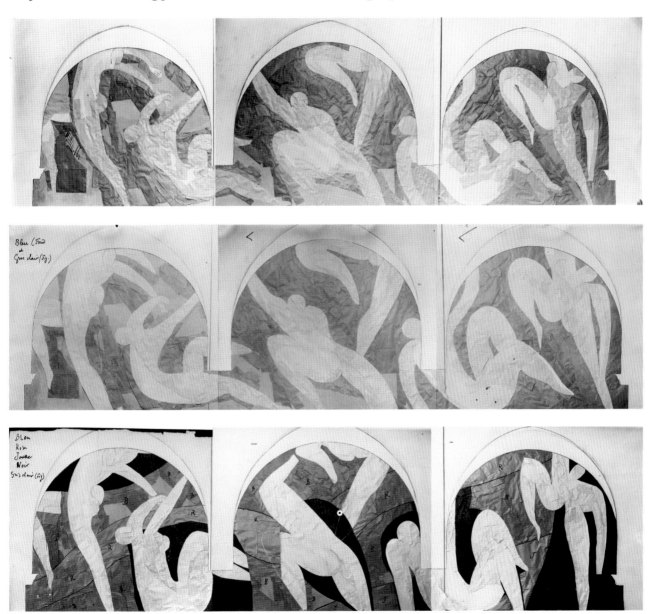

Matisse's technique was so unusual for the time that it bordered on the bizarre. "It was a strange sight," one visitor to the garage-studio recalled. "The whole of one wall was occupied by the cartoon, which was ingeniously composed of bits of coloured paper. These were pinned to the wall and could be shifted about like a gigantic jigsaw puzzle. On the floor were stacked piles of coloured papers. Matisse, armed with a piece of charcoal at the end of a long stick, would walk up and down in front of the cartoon and draw outlines of the changes he wished to make and a young woman whom one had not noticed before would step out, climb a ladder and rearrange the coloured papers."[76]

Although the poses of the figures in the early studies for the mural were similar to those in the Shchukin panel, they were necessarily more fragmented. Rather than fight against this fragmentation, Matisse decided to make it work for him. To deal with the lunettes and the vaulted ceiling, Matisse later said, "I made my figures larger than life-size, larger than the surfaces could contain. Thus there is half a body coming down from above. Another is half-length. Over an area which was not very wide, only 13 meters, I permitted the observer to see a much larger dance, because I used fragments."[77]

Matisse made a great effort to envisage how the picture would look when mounted at the Barnes Foundation. While the Shchukin *Dance* had been essentially an easel painting that could be hung anywhere, Matisse was very much aware that the Barnes panels were specifically tailored to the architecture and that in isolation they would be only "an architectural fragment."[78] "My aim," he told an interviewer, "has been to translate paint into architecture, to make of the fresco the equal of stone or cement."[79] Once he abandoned the matte, frescolike oil painting, he had to create the effect he desired by other means. To harmonize with the gray limestone of the building, the figures in the later versions of the mural were rendered in a cool, stony gray, while the background was eventually reduced to broad bands of black, pink, and blue. But he did not arrive at this color harmony immediately; in some of the early gouache renderings of the mural in progress, yellow is also employed in the background (see fig. 33). The essentially vertical rhythmic banding that Matisse finally settled on recalls the austere vertical black bands in the 1916 *Bathers by a River* (fig. 31), one of Matisse's most abstract early paintings. The effect of the near-vertical banding, the flatness, and the lack of modeling in both the Merion and Paris versions of the Barnes mural allow the painting itself to become an architectural element within the broader architectural complex of the building.

Because of the design of the building, the murals would also be seen against the light, but in the end Matisse felt that he had made the most of the situation: "The spaces between the doors are about two meters wide. I made use of the contrast created by these spaces; I used them to create correspondences with the forms in the ceiling.... Thus I displaced the contrast. Instead of making it between the bright doors and the spaces in between,

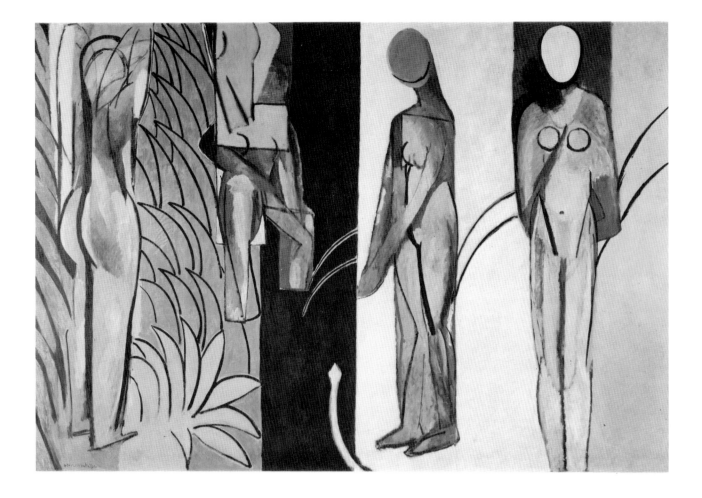

I put it up in the ceiling so that my very strong contrast united the whole panel, doors and spaces."[80] Although the frosted glass in the panes above the doors is nearly opaque, Matisse seems to have considered the effect of the sky and of greenery outside on the colors of the mural, perhaps because the doors were frequently left open in the fall, and Matisse almost certainly saw them that way when he first visited Merion. He frequently remarked that he considered the colors of the sky and garden as a kind of chromatic complement to his composition. And although Barnes refused to install transparent glass panes above the doors, Matisse persisted in calling attention to the important role that the outdoor colors played in his conception of the mural—much as he later would consider the absence of red in the chapel at Vence an essential part of the color scheme there, for the red was meant to exist "by reaction in the mind of the observer."[81] The colors he chose for the mural stood in sharp contrast to the outdoor greens and so helped create an ethereal ambience—an unearthly space set apart from nature.

Matisse had based the general movement of the figures in the early stages of the mural on the clockwise, right-to-left motion of the Shchukin painting. This is apparent in the numerous drawings he did for the composition and also in small gouaches that reflect various stages of the composi-

31. *Bathers by a River*, 1909, 1913, and 1916. Oil on canvas, 259.7 x 389.9 cm

The Art Institute of Chicago, Charles H. and Mary F. S. Worcester Collection

tion in progress, and in which the evolution from a flowing horizontal movement to a more geometrical and vertical division of the compositional elements is evident. This progression is documented in photographs that Matisse had taken of the composition while he was working on it, and which he seems to have used as the basis for his gouache renderings of different stages of it (figs. 28–30, 32–35). In the early stages the figures are strikingly abstracted and flattened—sometimes virtually splayed out across the surface—and the background has an undulating flow. Only after much struggle was Matisse able to find a means of harmonizing his composition with what he perceived as the demands of the architectural setting.

32. *Rendering of Barnes Mural in Progress,* 1931. Gouache on paper, 14 x 39 cm
Musée Matisse, Nice

33. *Rendering of Barnes Mural in Progress,* 1931. Gouache on paper, 35.6 x 64.1 cm
The Barnes Foundation, Merion, Pennsylvania

MATISSE: THE DANCE

Matisse's struggle to achieve an architectural painting, despite the difficulties posed by the architecture itself, was a subject that continued to preoccupy him long after he finished the mural. "How is it possible, without moving a stone, to make a large [unfavorable] part of the architecture favorable to a decorative painting?" Matisse later wrote in a notebook.

I had the honor to be chosen by Dr. Barnes to decorate the lunettes of the ceiling in the main hall of his Foundation. This surface [not being very favorable] was placed against the light above three very large, entirely glassed-in doors that are six meters high, dazzlingly bright, filling the whole wall and lighting up the whole room. Only the part of the ceiling situated above them, and which was the area to be painted, was entirely in shadow, as a result of the violent contrast. Having carefully observed these particular lighting conditions, I returned to Nice to execute the painting, thirteen meters long and more than three meters high. I worked on this for three years, constantly moving around 11 flat tinted shapes, a bit the way one moves around the pieces during a game of checkers (I [should] add that these shapes were pieces of colored paper) until I found an arrangement that satisfied me completely. It was when I saw the decoration in place at the foundation that I understood that during its execution I had been guided by the necessity of giving my painting the visibility that the architectural setting denied it. In effect, the two large surfaces of absolute

34. *Rendering of Barnes Mural in Progress,* 20 February 1932. Gouache on paper, 28 x 76 cm
Private collection

35. Photograph of *Paris Dance Mural* in progress, 20 February 1932
The Barnes Foundation, Merion, Pennsylvania

black came to be placed just above the two panels [of wall] that separate the three glass doors. The black surfaces of the spaces between the doors form a contrast, the strongest in the whole wall, lifting it, sufficiently overcoming the action of the light from the two doors which could have made my decoration impossible to see.[82]

As it turned out, Matisse's strategy for dealing with the problems inherent in the architecture and the space for the mural had to be implemented more than once. For the shapes and dimensions mapped out on the canvases he was working on did not conform to the dimensions of the space for which they were being designed. ▪ⁱ

A COSTLY
MISTAKE

BARNES, WHO WAS WORKING on his book about Matisse, wrote on 21 October 1931 to ask whether the mural was sufficiently advanced for him to see it in the artist's studio that December, so that he could illustrate and discuss it in the book, for which he hoped it would be the frontispiece. "The question is not whether it is completely finished, but let me know if its form is sufficiently advanced to permit me to analyze it from the point of view of its general plan of construction, and from certain other important aspects, such as the organization of the colors, themes of contrasts, the drawing, the decorative form, etc."[83]

Matisse hastened to reply in the negative. He did not want Barnes to know that the "painting" was in fact at that time composed of numerous pieces of cut paper, and that after a false start he was not as far along with the composition as he had hoped to be. On 6 November he wrote to say that he could not accommodate Barnes "until my work is finished. You will understand, since you know that I am working from morning to night, my imagination constantly active. I am distancing myself from everything that can distract me, and I hope to continue so right to the end of my work in complete liberty. That is why I cannot give you an idea of the composition reserving for myself the possibility of changing things until the last day, if I feel the possibility of giving the decoration greater fullness or expression."[84]

At the end of November Matisse wrote to his son Pierre, telling him, "My work goes as well as possible but it is quite long—even though I have been able to furnish my panels with unity and have pushed the design very far in the sense that is necessary. I have now 'worked' with some blue paper for the background and gray for the figures in a way to be able to have it painted when all will be well fixed. *(But it is necessary not to say anything about this).*"[85]

Matisse's concern about Barnes discovering the unorthodox technique that he was using was no doubt related to his growing awareness of Barnes' capriciousness. He had especially good reason to worry about how the hard-headed Barnes might react if he found out that he had paid for two-thirds of a painting that so far had virtually no paint on its surface!

When Barnes came to France in January 1932, he still had not seen the work in progress. He and Matisse met in Paris, and they compared the dimensions that they were working with, in preparation for eventually mounting the finished work on temporary stretchers so it could be shown at the Galeries Georges Petit in Paris before being sent to America. The exhibition of the work in Paris was very important to Matisse. According to an article in the *New York Times,* the galleries would be open until midnight "to enable all classes to view the canvas, and it will be specially lighted to insure losing none of its quality, both of these being daring innovations in gallery etiquette."[86] After meeting with Barnes, Matisse was horrified to find that there was a discrepancy between the widths of the spaces left for the pendentives in his composition and those that Barnes said existed on the wall of the building.

The misunderstanding about the measurements arose from several factors. To begin with, there was a small discrepancy between the architect's blueprints and the actual sizes of the irregularly shaped lunettes above the glass doors. This discrepancy was compounded by Matisse's misuse of the paper template that was supposed to have served to determine the exact size and shape of the canvases on which he would execute the work. To ensure that the murals would fit the space exactly, Barnes had had the template traced directly from the wall while Matisse was still in Merion.[87] Matisse had taken this template with him when he returned to France, and shortly afterward he had cabled Barnes for the architect's blueprints, in order to be doubly certain about the measurements.[88] The dimensions on the architect's blueprints were only slightly different from the template. But although the discrepancy was small, the presence of two different sets of dimensions added another element of confusion.

On 2 February Matisse cabled Barnes to inform him of this discrepancy and to request that the paper template, which had been returned to Merion, be sent to Nice as soon as possible so that he could compare his composition with it.[89] Barnes responded immediately, repeating that the dimensions on the architect's plans were *not* the same as those of the template, and that Matisse should ignore the architect's plans completely. Barnes affirmed that the dimensions of the template had to be correct, since they were taken directly from the wall, and that if they had been properly followed, the dimensions would be correct. As the template was then being used to guide the construction of the stretchers, Barnes said, it could not be returned for another two weeks.[90]

It soon became clear that Matisse had made a serious error in the measurements. On 22 February Barnes cabled Matisse confirming that the artist had been working from the wrong set of dimensions: he had followed the architect's plans rather than the template, and he had also overlooked two strips of paper that were to have been attached to the template. In fact, the pendentives under the lunettes were twice as wide as Matisse had supposed them to be. Barnes cabled: "YOU HAVE MADE AN ENORMOUS MISTAKE. REAL DIMENSIONS OF BASE OF LEFT PENDENTIVE ONE METER OF RIGHT PENDENTIVE ONE METER ELEVEN MILLIMETERS. TEMPLATE WE GAVE YOU HAD CORRECT DIMENSIONS. YOUR ERROR A RESULT OF YOUR OMISSION OF STRIP FORTY-FIVE CENTIMETERS BASE OF LEFT PENDENTIVE AND STRIP FORTY-FIVE CENTIMETERS SEVEN MILLIMETERS BASE OF RIGHT PENDENTIVE WHICH STRIPS WERE INCLUDED IN THE TEMPLATE

Matisse, stunned by the error he had made, realized almost immediately that it was too late for anything to be done about it. He cabled his regrets and said that he would soon start over again: "MY DEEPEST APOLOGIES AS NEW COMPOSITION IS NECESSARY I AM FINISHING PRESENT PANELS ALMOST FINISHED AND BEGINNING OVER ON NEW CANVASES SEND TEMPLATE NO NEED TO COME THANK YOU LETTER FOLLOWS."[92]

That very same day Barnes advised the Paris-based Swiss art dealer Georges Keller, who was then in New York, that "Matisse received our cablegram and replied that he would start an entirely new decoration as soon as the present one is finished, which he says will be very soon. I suppose he continues with the decoration in order to have it exhibited at the Galeries Georges Petit according to schedule." Barnes went on to say, "I am sure that Matisse would not like it known that he made an error, which he acknowledges in his cablegram to me; therefore, I ask that you say nothing about the matter."[93] Keller, who was actively involved in locating pictures for Barnes, replied immediately: "I am so sorry for you Matisse has got to start an entirely new decoration, since it is going to mean for you a new delay in getting the picture in Merion, but on the other hand if he has decided so it is certainly because there was no other way out, as we were all afraid when we first heard of his mistake."[94]

At this point the work in progress was still executed entirely in cut paper (with the first, later abandoned, painted version completely covered by the overlaid pieces of paper). What the composition looked like at this time is indicated in a gouache copy of it that Matisse made on 20 February 1932 (fig. 34). He apparently gave the copy to Barnes to reassure him about the aesthetic value (and the existence!) of the work when the two men met in Paris in early March.[95] In this gouache, the composition is the same as in a photograph of the actual canvases, dated "20/2 32" on the back (fig. 35). The design still has a strong lateral movement, and although the background is rendered as a series of oblique bands of color, the leaping and tumbling figures still seem to be inhabiting a somewhat tangible space. The figures are also much less integrally related to the architectural structure of the three arches than they became in the final composition.

For the next few weeks Matisse worked to perfect his composition, despite his knowledge that the dimensions were wrong and that he would have to start all over again. The work was photographed at least twice, around 29 February and on 8 March (figs. 36–37). In these two versions the compositions become more agitated and are given a tumbling motion that already seems to anticipate certain aspects of the *Merion Dance Mural.*

Matisse was deeply concerned about the future of the project. Barnes still did not know that the composition was rendered only in cut paper, and Matisse's promise to start a second mural brought up the awkward question of what would become of the first one. Moreover, he had already received two-thirds of the money for the mural, which he was in no posi-

36. Photograph of *Paris Dance Mural* in progress, c. 29 February 1932

The Barnes Foundation, Merion, Pennsylvania

37. Photograph of *Paris Dance Mural* in progress, 8 March 1932

The Barnes Foundation, Merion, Pennsylvania

tion to return should the situation with Barnes deteriorate that far.

On 26 February, Pierre Matisse wrote to his parents from New York on the eve of Barnes' departure for Europe to see the artist. From this letter it is clear that Matisse's technique was still a closely guarded secret. "I have naturally said nothing about the fashion in which Papa is working, I mean the cuttings of paper," Pierre said. He also recounted how deeply affected Barnes was by the mistake in the measurements: he had gone so far as to say that "it was the greatest tragedy of his life." Pierre also informed his parents that Keller

> is wondering what is going to happen to the present decoration, which he thinks is almost finished. This question must certainly be preoccupying Barnes. If he asks about buying more than the one that Papa must redo, calculate your price well—I mean don't...ask too much money. And I would pay attention not to let Keller-Bignou [at the time, Barnes' main Paris dealers] get too involved in this question of the decoration—remember also that Barnes repeats many things in a wrong or distorted way. Don't let Keller see the present decoration if this is possible....
>
> Keller's reflection: Barnes will not put up with the existence of another decoration similar to his own. Moreover he cannot ask the artist to just get rid of the first decoration. Make Barnes promise to repeat nothing of what you say together, you know that once his head is turned by someone he repeats everything. You could send him a telegram on the boat asking that he come alone to Nice.[96]

A week later Pierre wrote again, saying that when Barnes left for Europe he had been very disquieted about what was going to happen to the decoration that was already nearly finished.

He is afraid that later people are going to say that the more beautiful decoration is not the one he has, and moreover he seems not to want to lose
the magnificent and advantageous bargain that he has made paying only
X.... However it would not astonish me if he had an idea in his head
behind all of this and already had a proposition to be made. He insists a lot
on the responsibility of the Painter.... He accumulates all sorts of reasons
to show how much the artist owes him and all of the annoyances that his
error has given him. I am afraid that he might adopt a somewhat brutal
attitude in the exercise of what he will judge to be his rights. He is perhaps
afraid about one trying to get the upper hand on the price of the two
decorations in case he wishes to buy the first.... He is also going to have
Bignou and Keller behind his back, who can take advantage of this to turn
him toward affairs that are more profitable for them.[97]

As it turned out, however, Barnes did not come to Nice to see the
mural. Instead he and Matisse met in Paris, and it was agreed that Matisse
would continue with another version of the mural. No decision was made
about the disposition of the work that was already in Matisse's studio.

That summer Barnes wrote Matisse a detailed letter, with diagrams,
concerning the dimensions of the template and the necessary adjustments
of the dimensions previously agreed on, so that new canvases could be
stretched.[98] By the beginning of July Matisse had begun work on the
second set of three canvases. ▪

A NEW START

WHEN MATISSE BEGAN WORK on the new canvases in July 1932, he reconceived not only the physical composition but also the expressive feeling of the work. He also became more interested in keeping a record of the work in progress. Matisse had had some of the earlier versions of the mural composition photographed while the work was in progress (see figs. 24–25, 28–30, 35–37). But now he arranged for the photographer to come photograph the mural whenever he felt he had brought it to a certain stage of resolution. Although he had sometimes had works photographed while in progress before this, he had never done it as systematically as he did during the Barnes mural project and in the years just after it.[99]

For the new version he began by drawing directly on the large canvases in charcoal, without much preliminary planning (see fig. 43). During the course of its execution, he made some small compositional studies (figs. 38–41), but many fewer than when he had begun the first version. To achieve the monumental effect he was after, he felt that a certain kind of direct physical contact with the canvas was necessary. The composition of the mural, he later said, "is the result of the physical encounter between the artist and fifty-two square meters of surface that the artist had to take possession of, and not by the modern procedure of blowing up a composition more or less mechanically on a surface a certain number of times larger by means of tracings. A man with a searchlight who follows an airplane in the immensity of the sky does not move across it in the same way

38. *Study for Merion Dance Mural Composition*, 1932. Pencil on paper, 26.9 x 80.8 cm

Musée Matisse, Nice

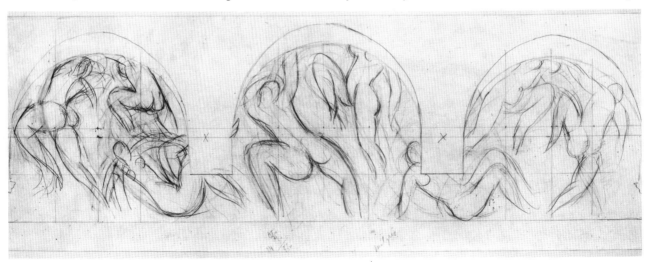

39. *Study for Merion Dance Mural Composition,* 1932. Pencil on paper, 30.2 x 79.8 cm

Musée Matisse, Nice

40. *Study for Left Panel of Merion Dance Mural Composition,* 1932. Pencil on paper, 25.8 x 33.2 cm

Musée Matisse, Nice

41. *Study for Merion Dance Mural Composition,* 1932. Pencil on paper, 20.7 x 53.5 cm

Musée Matisse, Nice

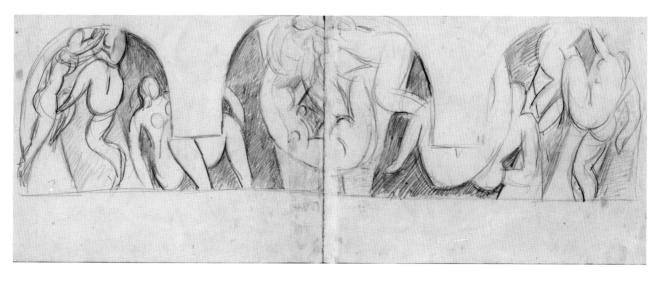

as an aviator."[100] The drawing style he employed to set the forms on the new canvases was extremely free and vigorous. The figures were highly simplified and had a linear purity similar to that of the Mallarmé etchings he had been working on for the past year or so.

In fact, the Mallarmé etchings seem to have served Matisse well in his studies for the mural. He employed a similarly simplified drawing style in both projects, and even some of the poses of specific figures are related. The leaping female figure that illustrates "Le Guignon" (fig. 42), for example, is closely related to the figure at the extreme left of the *Paris Dance Mural,* and several other figures in the Mallarmé book seem to have served as points of departure for the figures in the *Merion Dance Mural.* Moreover, the erotic overtones of the Merion mural are clearly related to the Mallarmé book.

Although Matisse began work on the new set of large canvases during the summer of 1932, he did not give them his full attention until after the publication of the Mallarmé book on 25 October. Shortly after he took up the mural again he engaged a new assistant, perhaps to placate his wife, who seems to have become increasingly resentful of Lisette's presence.[101]

Matisse's new assistant was Lydia Delectorskaya, an attractive young Russian émigrée, and her arrival was an important event for Matisse. In the ensuing years Lydia became his principal model and secretary. Eventually she displaced Amélie Matisse, and after Matisse and his wife were legally separated Lydia remained his close companion for the rest of his life.[102]

From the beginning of his work on the new version of the mural (State I; fig. 43), Matisse conceived of it in terms of eight rather than six figures, and as a composition that had three separate centers, in keeping with the much wider pendentives that separated the three lunettes. Matisse was concerned about how the mural would look when viewed within the relatively high and narrow space of the foundation's main gallery. Now, to better accommodate his composition to the conditions in which it would actually be seen, he changed its structure. Instead of having the figures move laterally across all three canvases, he centered them within the individual panels. In early November he wrote to his son Pierre that

> since the 20th of last month, that is two weeks, I've worked on the decoration, I've set the drawing. It's going very well and I perceive that I have greatly profited from the 1st one, and from my illustrations of Mallarmé. But the problem is (perhaps luckily because this is a new problem) that it is necessary to have three centers of composition. Because of the vaults one can't see the whole decoration at once—except from very far and through the halls—and I am conscious this time that to judge the decoration [as it will be seen] in Merion there are no more than 10 or 15 meters to back up away from it. I am very happy with the 1st decorat[ion], which I will execute after the 2nd one.[103]

It was at this point that Matisse really began to gain momentum with his work on the new version. "My decoration is going very well," he wrote to Pierre at the end of the month, "and although I have only been working

42. *Le Guignon,* summer 1931–autumn 1932. Page 8 from *Poésies* by Stéphane Mallarmé, Lausanne, Albert Skira & Cie Editeurs, 1932. Etching, printed in black, 32.2 x 25.3 cm

The Museum of Modern Art, New York, The Louis E. Stern Collection

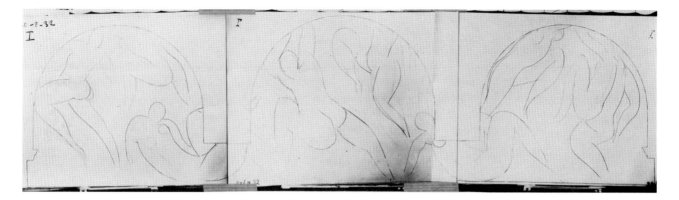

43. Photograph of *Merion Dance Mural* in progress, State I, 20 August 1932

The Barnes Foundation, Merion, Pennsylvania

on it 1 month, I am very far along with it—the first has helped me enormously."[104] Matisse was still quite concerned about how clearly the mural could be seen from the second-floor loggia, and he had asked Barnes to send sketches that would show whether any of it would be blocked by the loggia arches. These sketches were to be done by the Pinto brothers, who were then students at the foundation, but Matisse grew impatient and asked Pierre to intervene.

Toward the end of the month Pierre wrote to his father, providing him with this information: "Knowing what you wanted I indicated to them how to determine the part hidden by the curves of the arches [of the loggia]— and their form." In his letter Pierre sketched the position of the loggia in relation to the mural and informed his father that since the entire mural would be visible from the center of the loggia, and virtually the whole mural would be visible from its extremities, there was no reason to worry about an obstructed view.[105] Matisse could continue with the composition as he had already developed it.

IN THE EARLIEST STAGE OF THE NEW COMPOSITION, there was still a certain lateral flow in the movement of the figures across the three separate panels. The reclining figures under the pendentives were composed as part of an overall arabesquelike motion that was set in counterpoint to the architectural design, rather than in direct structural accord with it. And the leaping figure at the far left still moved to the extreme left edge of the picture, as in the Shchukin *Dance*.

Eventually, however, the organization became more internally contained and more clearly segmented within the separate panels (State IV; fig. 44). The leftmost figure begins to turn back into the picture space, and there is a distinct separation between the pairs of leaping figures within the lunettes and the reclining figures fixed under the downward thrust of the pendentives. At this fourth stage the pendentive figures are first clearly turned in opposite directions, one seen from the front, the other from behind, in a direct echo of the two reclining figures in the *Bonheur de vivre*.

Shortly afterward Matisse made the pairs of dancing figures within the lunettes even more violently active (State VII; fig. 45). At this stage of the

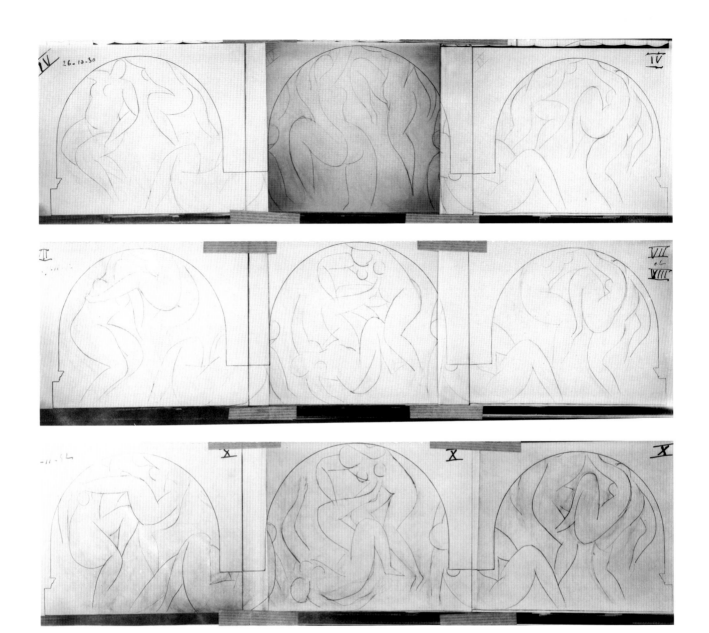

44. Photograph of *Merion Dance Mural* in progress, State IV, 26 October 1932

The Barnes Foundation, Merion, Pennsylvania

45. Photograph of *Merion Dance Mural* in progress, State VII, 29 October 1932

The Barnes Foundation, Merion, Pennsylvania

46. Photograph of *Merion Dance Mural* in progress, State X, 9 November 1932

The Barnes Foundation, Merion, Pennsylvania

composition, the dance begins to verge on a *lutte d'amour,* or battle of love. The physical violence of the figures in the next few stages is remarkable, and quite unprecedented in Matisse's earlier work. This is especially marked in the center panel, where the figures seem virtually to be spinning in a kind of Dionysian frenzy (State X; fig. 46). The composition of the central panel at this stage clearly anticipates the figures in one of Matisse's most violently sexual images, *Nymph in the Forest (La verdure),* which was begun a few years later and reworked over a long period of time.[106]

As Matisse modified his composition, he experimented with different kinds of poses, including intensely foreshortened ones (States IX–XII; see fig. 47). At one point he even added leaf forms in the background (States

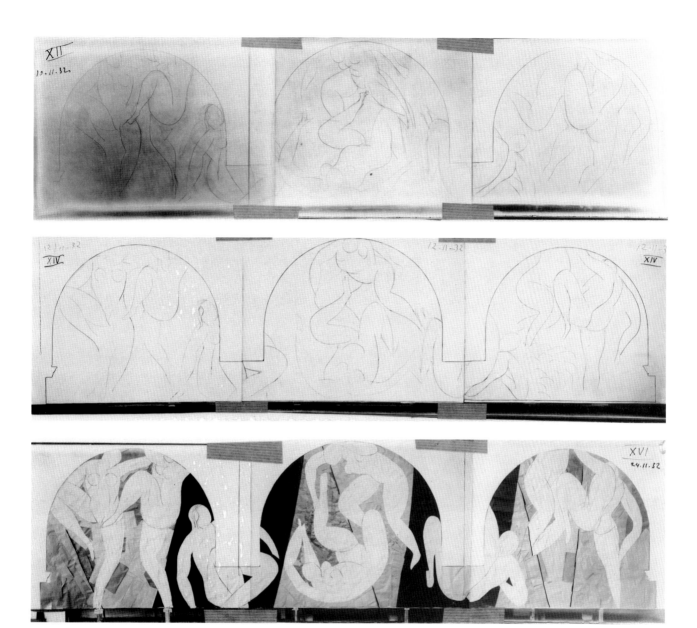

XIV–XV; see fig. 48), similar to those in an early stage of the 1916 *Bathers by a River*. By 24 November he had covered the entire surface of the picture space with colored papers (State XVI; fig. 49). He then began to emphasize the oblique movements in the background, which became increasingly complex as the work progressed. By 14 December he was already close to the final composition (State XIX; fig. 50). After 20 December, when the figures were fairly well resolved, he devoted more attention to adjusting the forms in the background. Early in January 1933 he broadened the poses of the pendentive figures to relate them better to their architectural function of seeming to bear some of the weight of the arches.

At this time Barnes had not yet seen the mural and still did not know that Matisse was working with colored paper rather than directly with

47. Photograph of *Merion Dance Mural* in progress, State XII, 10 November 1932

The Barnes Foundation, Merion, Pennsylvania

48. Photograph of *Merion Dance Mural* in progress, State XIV, 12 November 1932

The Barnes Foundation, Merion, Pennsylvania

49. Photograph of *Merion Dance Mural* in progress, State XVI, 24 November 1932

The Barnes Foundation, Merion, Pennsylvania

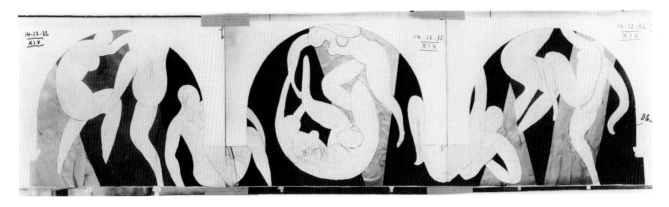

50. Photograph of *Merion Dance Mural* in progress, State XIX, 14 December 1932

The Barnes Foundation, Merion, Pennsylvania

paint. Barnes was impatient to view it and wanted to stop off in Nice when he came to Europe in January. Matisse was reluctant, but Barnes persuaded him to come to Palma de Mallorca in mid-January, when the Barneses would be there on their way to Spain.[107] Matisse acquiesced, apparently because he saw this as a way of firming up his personal relationship with Barnes before showing him the cut-paper mural compositions. After a rough boat trip from Villefranche, during which he was quite seasick and caught cold, he arrived in Palma on Saturday evening 14 January, a day and a half ahead of Barnes.

While waiting for Barnes, Matisse was suddenly struck with deep anxiety and self-doubt. "I don't know if I have done the right thing in accepting his invitation," he wrote his son Pierre, "because I dread this week that is to be spent with him so nervous and bustling—I am very tired at this moment." He was anxious about Barnes' reaction to the mural: "I am afraid that he will return [to Nice] with me because of the revolution in Spain.... First I want to rework my picture before he sees it. I should return to America leaving from Villefranche on the 'Rex' in February—I'm not sure of the exact date—he is arriving tomorrow after having taken Madame Barnes to Gibraltar."[108]

By the time Barnes arrived that Monday, Matisse was feeling so poorly that he left by the very same boat that Barnes had just come on, after spending only a very brief time with him. Matisse returned to France via the faster (and more expensive) overland route by train and was in Nice the

51. Photograph of *Merion Dance Mural* in progress, State XXIV, 25 January 1933

The Barnes Foundation, Merion, Pennsylvania

next day. He immediately began to make alterations in the composition, in anticipation of Barnes' visit (State XXIV; fig. 51). He increased the upward thrust of the figures in the two outside panels and refined the drawing of the limbs of the figures, giving the composition more stability and a greater emphasis on vertical rhythms.[109]

A week later, on 24 January, Barnes came to Nice and saw the mural for the first time. Much to Matisse's relief, he was enthusiastic about what he saw. He was not disturbed by the cut-paper technique and even told Matisse to finish the picture as it was. "A picture," he said, "is never finished," and he asserted that the composition of the panels was already sufficiently developed to be considered done. Matisse, however, decided to continue, uncertain about how much more time he would need. He thought that he would be able to finish the mural in a week or so, but he ended up working on it for the next two months.[110]

Matisse was relieved by Barnes' positive reaction to the mural, but he was also beginning to lose patience with the collector. Barnes' rough manner ruffled the Frenchman's sense of decorum, and Matisse began to find him extremely tiresome. He was especially irritated by a note that Barnes had written to him when he arrived in Nice, in which he had employed the condescending salutation, "Mon cher enfant." He was further exasperated by Barnes' stinginess, by the boorishness he had displayed in drinking too much wine and staying too late when invited to dinner, and by his asking indiscreet questions about Matisse's finances.[111]

Matisse took up work on the mural again right after Barnes left (State XXV; fig. 52),[112] and revised it intensively for the next two months, making it more linear and giving greater emphasis to the way the background shapes are played against the gestures of the figures. In the final stages he distinctly lowered the emotional pitch of the work, following his ideal of creating a decorative ensemble that would hold its own with the masterpieces in the gallery but not overwhelm them.[113] In mid-February he wrote Pierre that he believed Barnes would be amazed by how much he had changed it, and by how much he had improved it.[114]

By 21 February Matisse had begun what he hoped would be the final phase of work on the cut-paper composition of the mural, and he hired the

52. Photograph of *Merion Dance Mural* in progress, State XXV, 26 January 1933

The Barnes Foundation, Merion, Pennsylvania

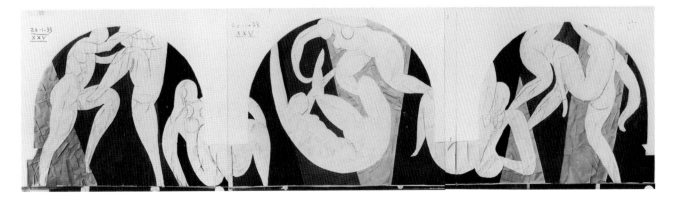

housepainter Goyo to help with the physical labor involved.[115] On 24 February Matisse's friend the painter Simon Bussy came to his studio to see the work in progress and to reassure him about it.[116] But on 27 February Matisse wrote to his son Pierre that he still had a lot more to do.

> My decoration which [Barnes] found to be finished, I continue to work on, despite thinking that I was at the end. It has after all gained a good deal of amplitude since his departure. Despite everything that it is costing me, I cannot, in any case, help but go right to the end of my idea. I am at this moment very tired—I am recovering a little—and I think I have enough energy to go right to the end…. When you see Barnes, ask him to show you the 28 photos of the panel giving its history and development—don't fix yourself on the last one because it has developed further—Barnes forgets perhaps what he has said: the principal condition is that you make it *as if for yourself*.[117]

Try as he might, Matisse could not keep from constantly reworking the composition, which he saw even in his dreams. According to Lydia Delectorskaya, Matisse would indicate changes in the composition with charcoal, and while she was cutting and moving the pieces of paper, he would go out for walks with his dog, sometimes stopping at a local shooting arcade. The only time when he was not thinking of his mural, he told her, was when he concentrated on aiming his rifle at the target.[118] On 7 March he wrote to Bussy, who had been to his studio to see the mural only a fortnight earlier, "I would like to go to warm myself with your friendship, and to tell you about the ups and downs of my work, which is still developing apace toward the goal that I hold myself to, that is to say decorative painting as an integral part of the architecture. However, the end is near—win or lose."[119]

But in mid-March Matisse was still putting the finishing touches on the composition. He wrote to Pierre on 13 March:

> I cannot tell you when I will go to New York for [the installation of] the decoration because I am not finished composing it. I think that it will not be for several weeks—maybe a month, and it still has to be painted, which I think will only take a week or two—so that I think that I won't be able to leave before 6 weeks from now—or in 2 months.
>
> I am glad to have continued working on it after Barnes left, because it is much better. One has to be careful about things that one thinks adequate but which can end up leaving you remorseful when it concerns a piece of work like this.[120]

The following week Goyo came to the studio to begin preparations for the final painting of the panels.[121] Although Matisse had planned to exhibit the mural at the Galeries Georges Petit in Paris, just as he had arranged to do with the first version a year earlier, he was beginning to doubt that he would finish the work in time. On 30 March he wrote to his daughter to say that the actual painting of the panels by Goyo was taking longer than he had expected, and that all areas except the blacks were going to need two coats of paint. The painting process would not be finished before 13 April, and the panels would not be dry enough to ship until the end of that month.[122]

Eventually he had to abandon his plan to exhibit the mural in Paris.

As the color was laid down, Matisse also found that the effect of the paint on the canvas was less matte than it had been on the paper, and that he would have to add linear accents in charcoal to enhance the articulation of the figures. "It is probably necessary for me to rework the figures and indicate accents in charcoal in order to underline certain forms," he wrote Marguerite. "I see this increasingly and very clearly. While Goyo paints I am studying that. The accent of the thigh (in charcoal) which seemed strong, is taking on more and more quality. It is going to be my point of departure."[123] In fact, when Goyo had finished applying the paint, Matisse felt that the surface was too impersonal. He therefore repainted the contours himself and added areas of shadow to enliven the composition.[124]

MATISSE PLANNED AND SUPERVISED the crating of the three canvases, which he was going to take with him when he sailed for New York. Toward the end of April work on the panels was finished, and Matisse cabled Barnes to tell him that he had booked passage on the *Rex* for 11 May. Because the dollar was losing value against the franc, he sent a second cable on 21 April, asking Barnes to convert the last payment for the murals into francs as soon as possible. Barnes immediately replied that he would do so, but two days later he sent another cable with the instructions: "DO NOT CUT THE DECORATION BRING IT IN ONE PIECE."[125]

At this point Matisse, exhausted and extremely anxious about how Barnes was going to react to the finished work, took fright. He misinterpreted Barnes' cable as a sign that Barnes wanted to see only one of the panels in order to judge it before he made the last payment for the entire work. As Matisse was all too well aware, the letter of agreement stipulated that the third payment would be made "when the paintings are installed in our gallery."[126] Matisse cabled back immediately: "DO NOT UNDERSTAND CLARIFY." As his anxiety mounted, he began to remember all the difficulties he had had with Barnes over the past couple of years, especially during his recent trip to Mallorca and Barnes' visit to Nice. In particular he recalled Barnes' cool remark to Mrs. Barnes when they had come to see the mural in Nice: "If I don't like it, I'll just put it aside."[127] Anxious not to complicate things even further, Matisse tried to cancel his cable, but it had already been transmitted. So instead he sent another cable with a single word: "UNDERSTOOD."[128]

The very next day Matisse wrote to Pierre, explaining his doubts. After thinking the matter over, he decided that his request for the rest of the money before Barnes had seen the panels had cut Barnes to the quick, since Barnes wanted to reserve the sole right to pass final judgment on the mural. Matisse also recalled the recent visit of a student at the Barnes Foundation, who had spent a couple of hours watching him work on the last stages of the mural. The student had been surprised by the fact that Matisse had engaged an assistant for the actual painting of the picture and by the extreme flatness of the work. Matisse thought the student might have described the work to Barnes as being in a "poster style."

But despite Matisse's fears about Barnes' possible adverse reaction to the mural, he himself remained confident about its quality. Come what may, he wrote, "I am happy with my work and can't wait to see it in place —with the glass doors below for which [the panels] have been made—one should see the sky [and] the greenery through them—when one is in the loggia on the first floor."[129]

Matisse's fears were unfounded. The three panels were packed in crates and accompanied him on the *Rex*.[130] He arrived in New York as scheduled on Thursday, 11 May 1933, and was driven to Merion the next day by Pierre. The truck with the canvases arrived in Merion late that same afternoon, having taken a circuitous route to avoid low bridges and trolley wires. That very evening the crates were unpacked, and the canvases were laid out in the gallery, ready to be stretched the next day.

As is apparent from letters Matisse wrote to his wife and daughter, he and Barnes had a rough time of it.[131] The two men had already begun to get on each other's nerves earlier in the year. To make matters worse, when Matisse arrived Barnes was extremely upset about the poor reception of his book on the artist, which had been published a few months earlier and had been the subject of a harshly critical review.[132] Matisse, for his part, was physically and emotionally exhausted by the demands of finishing the mural and by his anxiety about what Barnes would think of it. He was also quite unhappy about Barnes' refusal to remove the two large paintings that were placed directly under the mural panels, his own 1913 *Seated Riffian* and Picasso's *Peasants* of 1906 (see fig. 53). He felt that they undermined the mural panels by creating an unfortunate contrast with the mural's relative emotional coolness and upset the fine distinctions between mural decoration and easel painting that had so preoccupied him in recent months.[133] He was also disturbed by Barnes' unwillingness to remove the sculptured frieze just below the mural, which in Matisse's opinion detracted from the panels and interfered with the way they related to the architecture.

Matisse was further upset by Barnes' refusal to replace the frosted glass panes above the french doors that were just below the mural with clear glass, so that the outdoor greenery would be more visible. From the beginning Matisse had considered the view through the windows as part of the ensemble. In 1931 Alfred Barr had remarked on Matisse's enthusiastic acceptance of "the difficulty of relating the decorations to the luminous green of the grass and trees seen through the windows."[134] Just a few weeks before the mural was installed, Matisse had been particularly enthusiastic about the way the landscape would be played off against the mural and had written to Pierre about "the sky [and] the greenery" that should be visible. On the eve of his departure to install the mural, he had told an interviewer about his idea that the mural would create "the sky for the garden one sees through the doors."[135]

On Saturday, when the time came to stretch the first canvas, Barnes wanted the work done by Albert Nulty, his former chauffeur and handyman, who had been put in charge of caring for the foundation's paintings. But Matisse insisted on nailing the first canvas to the stretcher himself.

It was then that the strain of the past several months took its toll. After a couple of hours of work, Matisse had what Barnes described as "a mild heart attack." Barnes responded by giving him some whiskey and making him rest, and by Barnes' own account Matisse "was all right in an hour or two."[136]

That night Barnes called in a friend who was a heart specialist. As Barnes explained to Pierre Matisse two days later, the specialist examined Matisse and "found that he has a disturbance of the heart and circulation. He said that your father is in need of absolute rest for a long period and must not do any work whatsoever…. There is no immediate cause for alarm but when a man reaches your father's age it is necessary for him to readjust his life to changed conditions which advancing years bring on."[137]

By Sunday Matisse was feeling better, and he supervised the stretching

53. *Merion Dance Mural* installed at The Barnes Foundation.

The Barnes Foundation, Merion, Pennsylvania

and mounting of the other two canvases. By Matisse's own account, everyone was very moved by the effect that the mural created. Matisse called it "my masterpiece," and the day after it was installed Barnes gathered all the foundation's students together in the main gallery and gave a three-hour lecture about it.[138]

In fact, just what brought about the heart trouble—which was more likely what we would now call a stress attack—is not entirely clear. Matisse and Barnes had apparently exchanged some heated words about how they should go about stretching and mounting the canvases, and the tension that had been building between them had come to a head. In his carefully worded letter to Pierre Matisse, Barnes remarked that "when your father arrived on Friday I noticed that he looked tired and naturally was excited.... he insisted on nailing the first of the canvases on the chassis in spite of the fact that we have an expert with long experience in doing such work." Barnes also went out of his way to ensure that Pierre understood that the heart specialist had said that Matisse "must avoid social engagements of all kind while in this country and advised that he return home as soon as he can in order to have the absolute rest which one can obtain only in their own surroundings."[139] Although Barnes' concern for Matisse was no doubt genuine, it is also conceivable that he wanted Matisse to see as few people as possible, and thus to say as little as possible about either Barnes or the foundation.

Matisse was picked up by Pierre very early on Tuesday morning and taken back to New York. Aside from what he told his son, and what he wrote to his wife and daughter that same day, he kept his thoughts about Barnes to himself. He never did tell his wife about the "heart attack," out of concern for her own fragile health. From New York he wrote to Amélie that both he and Barnes were very pleased with the effect that the mural created, and that "the whole ceiling came alive and the radiation from the canvas goes right down to the bottom of the wall. Seen from the floor, you would believe you were in a cathedral."[140]

His public stance was that he was exhausted but triumphant. "My decoration is in place," he wrote to Bussy, with an understandable lack of modesty. "It has a splendour that one can't imagine unless one sees it—because both the whole ceiling and its arched vaults come alive through radiation and the main effect continues right down to the floor.... I am profoundly tired but very pleased. When I saw the canvas put in place, it was detached from me and became part of the building, and I completely forgot the past, it became like a living thing. It was like a real *birth* in which the mother becomes detached from the past pain."[141]

In public both Matisse and Barnes continued to praise each other and the mural. "J'étais ravi," Matisse told Dorothy Dudley shortly after the mural was installed. "As soon as I saw the decoration in place, I felt that it was detached absolutely from myself, and that it took on a meaning quite different from what it had had in my studio, where it was only a painted canvas. There in the Barnes Foundation it became a rigid thing, heavy as stone, and one that seemed to have been spontaneously created at the same time with the building." According to Matisse, Barnes had said that the painting was "like the rose window of a cathedral," and Matisse himself referred to it as being "like a song that mounts to the vaulted roof."[142]

No public mention was made by either Barnes or Matisse about the heart trouble or about the tensions and resentments that had grown up between them. Still, both men nursed hard feelings. Although Matisse sent Barnes a telegram saying that he planned to return to Merion at the end of the week, he apparently never saw the mural again.[143] And he might not have been particularly welcome just then. Barnes was evidently displeased by the public attention Matisse was receiving, feeling that it was, after all, now *his* mural, even though Matisse had made it. For his part Matisse felt that Barnes had become dismissive once the mural was in place, and he found his patron's caprices and egotism unbearable, verging on madness.[144] Even worse, it now became clear that Barnes had no intention of opening his foundation to a wider public after the mural was installed. Quite the opposite: Barnes' passion for buying important pictures seemed to be matched only by his passion for excluding the public from seeing them.[145]

Although Barnes praised the mural in public, he seems to have been disappointed by it. According to Henry Hart, "Barnes was never completely satisfied with it, but he never told the artist so."[146] After the panels were installed, Barnes became markedly less enthusiastic about buying paintings by Matisse.[147]

Matisse was aware of Barnes' initial coolness toward the mural. In *The Art of Henri Matisse,* Barnes and de Mazia had included a chapter entitled, "Matisse's Rank as an Artist," in which they ranked Matisse highest among contemporary artists, but lower than all of the older masters he was compared to, including El Greco, Giorgione, Titian, and Renoir. Most stinging, no doubt, was the comparison with Giotto, which seems to reflect most directly Barnes' evaluation of the mural. "Matisse gets nothing at all of Giotto's deep mysticism," Barnes and de Mazia wrote, "and little or nothing of the human dignity of Giotto's figures. A group of figures in Giotto plays the rôle of a group not only plastically but as a human or dramatic assemblage, a religious procession, or a group of mourners; Matisse's groups are seldom much more than a set of pictorial units."[148] Even worse, the book described Matisse as someone who for all his intelligence "never loses his calculation, the sobriety of a judge or a banker, and with him creation is largely a matter of skilful and ingenious manipulation…. He has far too much insight, too great an interest in his world, to be a mere decorator, but it is impossible not to feel that he is interested less in objects for what they really are than in the ways in which they can be woven into decorative designs."[149] Just how hurt Matisse had been by this criticism is evident from his quick retort to Dorothy Dudley when she remarked of the murals that she had never seen "a thing so simple and so calculated."

"Calculated," Matisse replied, "is not the right word. For forty years I have worked without interruption; I have made studies and experiments. What I do now issues from the heart. All that I paint is produced that way. I feel it."[150]

Less than two weeks after the mural was installed, Matisse returned to France, ending his last trip to the United States. On the day he left he made a statement directly aimed at Barnes, telling an interviewer that "when a painting is finished, it's like a newborn child, and the artist himself must have time for understanding. How then, do you expect an amateur to understand that which the artist does not yet comprehend?"[151]

Although relations between Matisse and Barnes had cooled considerably, they stayed in touch and established a pattern of occasional but cordial communication. In January 1934 Barnes sent Matisse a card to say that a number of people had been by to see the mural and had praised it. Barnes noted that his own appreciation of the mural was "growing day by day because I see in it more and more of your artistic personality"—clearly implying that he had previously felt Matisse's artistic personality to be lacking in the mural.[152] Matisse responded cautiously to Barnes' card. He expressed his pleasure at hearing that the canvases had not been adversely affected by the humid summer weather. He then went on to say how pleased he was to hear about the positive role in "the spiritual life of the foundation, of this work that caused me so much travail." To which he could not refrain from adding that this was what he himself had "spontaneously" expected when the mural was installed the year before.[153]

Despite the cooling of their personal relationship, the two men seem to have benefited from their experiences with each other. As a result of his direct contact with Matisse, Barnes was later able to criticize scholars and museum directors with a stronger sense of authority about what the artist thought and felt. And Matisse had finally been able to work his way through the impasse in his painting and prepare for a breakthrough. In this process the still unfinished "first" version was to play an even more important role than the picture installed in Merion. ▪

A RETURN TO
SOURCES

WHEN MATISSE RETURNED to France in June 1933, he was exhaust-ed. "I am feeling better," he wrote to Bussy, "but I came back to Nice extremely tired, my heart strained. A long rest will put me back in shape—all the same, I've been specifically advised not to start on another project like this one. I'm incapable of doing anything right now, so it's not too difficult to resign myself to taking it easy....when I'm at the point of sinking into a depression I pull myself together by reminding myself of the complete success of that famous panel."[154] But his health continued to deteriorate. A few weeks later, he was immobilized by an attack of acute nephritis.

While Matisse was recovering, Etta Cone came to Nice with her broth-er's wife and children, and called on him. Although she had planned to leave the next day, he insisted that she stay long enough to see the first ver-sion of the mural, which was still at rue Désiré-Niel. "Matisse would not listen to my plan to leave Nice the next morning," Etta wrote her brother, explaining that the artist wanted her to see the mural. Matisse had decided that Etta Cone would be the perfect buyer for the still unfinished first version. She was one of his major collectors, she had sufficient financial resources, and she was planning to leave her entire collection to a museum. (Perhaps equally important to Matisse, Baltimore was close enough to Merion to cause Barnes some discomfort should the first version end up there. The fact that Matisse was considering such a proposition is a good indication of how he felt about Barnes at this time.) Although Etta wrote that it was "a wonderful production and Laura and the children got great pleasure from seeing it,"[155] she was nonetheless unable to buy it. Her nephew Edward later recalled that

> Matisse had insisted that we stay an extra day in Nice so that he could meet us, and so that we could all see the original version of his mural for the Barnes Collection. This was not yet finished, for in the course of painting it the artist had discovered that its dimensions were wrong. It was now housed in a sort of barn, awaiting completion; and Margot, who was to arrive the next day, would take us to see it. After that we were to pay our respects to him. For Aunt Etta this was a command, one that she gladly obeyed even though it meant totally abandoning our already battered schedule, and one in which we eagerly acquiesced.
>
> The mural—like the one at the Barnes Museum, a composition of huge dancing nudes, but stronger and less graceful—made a tremendous impression on all of us. Aunt Etta said simply, "Je suis comblée," and that expressed what we all felt. So it was with a real sense of the honor that

was bestowed on us that we paid our call on the master and his wife.

The apartment, with its red tile floors and sunny windows, was familiar from many paintings. Mme. Matisse, kind and motherly, greeted us warmly and plied us with tea until her husband was ready for us. He proved to be most genial, talking volubly about his recent kidney stones, the climates of France and North Carolina, and his hopes that the mural we had just seen might one day rest in a specially built Cone Museum. The doctor arrived and we had to leave, Aunt Etta's spirits only slightly dampened by the realization that even if she could some day afford the expense of granting Matisse's wish, she would probably lack the energy for such an undertaking.[156]

Although Matisse's doctor advised him to rest, he was anxious to work on the remaining version of the mural. Not long after Etta Cone's visit, he went over to the studio at rue Désiré-Niel and worked on it for an hour. At this time it was still composed entirely of cut and pinned paper, which completely covered the unfinished oil painting under it. He contented himself with redrawing some of the forms with chalk. "I couldn't resist the impulse," he wrote to Bussy, "and I reworked my first panel from top to bottom for an hour—fortunately in chalk, so nothing is irreversible. Don't worry, if I go back to it, it will be only for a day or two each week between working on the paintings I want to do."[157] Shortly afterward he left for Vittel where his physician had advised him to rest and take the cure.

When Matisse returned to Nice, he began to rework the mural composition, assisted by his daughter Marguerite. Although he had been told not to exert himself, he once again became absorbed by the problem of making the composition work in a flatter, more architectural, and more purely decorative way. Proceeding gradually at first, he altered the composition quite a bit, making it less fluid and less lateral, and emphasizing the structural relationships between the figures and the arches. Some of the figures were at first altered in a way that clearly reflects the composition of the Merion mural. This is especially evident in the second figure from the left, which was transformed from a seated to a tumbling figure; in an intermediate stage, it clearly resembled the lower figure in the central panel of the *Merion Dance Mural*. At this stage Matisse also introduced several arabesquelike movements into his composition. But after he had done so, he began to have second thoughts about the direction that the composition was taking, and he eventually went back to a conception closer to the way it was when he abandoned it in February 1932.

He wrote to his son Pierre in mid-October 1933

I am working on my decoration, which I am executing just as it was left a year ago, with its warrior character...reserving the right to return to this character. I have tried to push further—more space, etc. It did not go badly, after seven or eight sessions I understood that I was moving toward an undefined goal—which I saw in the character of the decoration in Merion—even better—but that I was losing the particular character that it had before I retouched it. I decided, courageously, to go back to where I was, and to stay there. I have the new canvases stretched, the papers assembled in little glued bands in such a way that I can move them onto the new canvases without them coming apart. But what work. I, who would like to paint some flowers, I have at least one good month to go, that would be 15 November. Then these canvases can dry quietly until the end of December, when they could be transported rolled up separately to my sculpture studio at Place Charles-Félix, be unrolled on the 5 meter wide wall there, like a curtain in a theater—with the large one behind and the two others in front, leaving a space of 15 centimeters between them, they can stay there until the Salon d'Automne, in 1 year.[158]

As he got back into the spirit of the work, he progressed more rapidly. "I was able to take up work on my panels again," he wrote Bussy a few days later. "The two panels, the one at the right and the one in the middle are standing, the cartoon applied, I am going to begin my tracing. For the third I have to wait two weeks until Guichardaz sends me the canvas. I am very happy to be able (not all alone) to triumph over the manual part of this work which I would very easily have abandoned without Marguerite's and your efforts."[159]

When Matisse brought his composition to a point where he was satisfied with it, he glued together the various areas of pinned paper and made tracings of the different parts, which could be used to transfer the entire composition to the new set of three canvases that he had ordered. When this process was completed, he rolled up the three canvases with the *Unfinished Dance Mural* painted on them—which for the past two years had been covered by the cut-paper composition—and stored them away. They remained lost from sight until they were rediscovered nearly sixty years later.

When the actual painting of the *Paris Dance Mural* was completed in November 1933, Matisse left it in the studio at rue Désiré-Niel to dry until the end of the year, when his lease on the studio ran out.[160] That December a group of students from the Barnes Foundation came to see this version of the mural, which Matisse persisted in calling "the first decoration,"[161] in part out of habit, in part so as not to arouse Barnes' ire by revealing that his was not the "definitive" version. Matisse's anger had by now cooled, and Barnes remained someone with whom he had good reason to stay on cordial terms. The two men kept in touch with each other, and Matisse continued, though unsuccessfully, to try to persuade Barnes to remove the *Seated Riffian* and *The Peasants* from below the mural.[162] Nor was he any more successful in persuading Barnes to open the foundation to a larger public or to install transparent glass panes below the mural so that the greenery and sky would be visible.

The inaccessibility of the Merion mural made Matisse all the more determined to place the recently finished "first" version in a public collection. In the spring of 1934 he sent his son Pierre color photographs of the mural, "so that if the occasion arises you can show it to museum people around New York...to whom you have spoken about it."[163] The following year he executed an aquatint copy of the new version of the mural, which could be used as a kind of visual prospectus for helping to sell it.[164] During the summer of 1936 Raymond Escholier, curator of the Musée du Petit Palais, negotiated the purchase of the mural by the city of Paris, with the intention of hanging it in the museum of modern art that was being built on the Avenue de Tokio.[165] The official acquisition by the Musée d'art moderne de la Ville de Paris was made in January 1937 with funds appropriated for the large 1937 International Exhibition in Paris.[166] Matisse had hoped to see his mural installed in a prominent place when the museum opened, but instead a blown-up version of Raoul Dufy's *Electricity* was installed in the gallery that Matisse had thought would be reserved for his mural.

Although this version of the mural remained in the museum's collection, it was not installed during Matisse's lifetime—a great disappointment to him. When the *Paris Dance Mural* was finally given a permanent display at the museum in 1977, the installation was so unsatisfactory that it evoked complaints from the Matisse family. The mural was cleaned, restored, and given a new installation in 1989.[167]

FOR THE IMAGERY OF THE BARNES MURAL, Matisse had returned to the most essential sources of his art. He himself was aware of the deep continuity that the dance theme represented in his art, and the broad flat areas of color in the Barnes murals also refer back to the stylistic breakthrough of the *Bonheur de vivre,* a work that had almost talismanic significance for Matisse. In that picture he had found an alternative to the spontaneous manner of his fauve paintings and for the first time fully asserted his gifts as a colorist.[168] Toward the end of his life Matisse reaffirmed the importance of this seminal early work within his overall development, when he told an interviewer that "from the *Bonheur de vivre*—I was thirty-five then—to this cut-out—I am eighty-two—I have not changed...because all this time, I have looked for the same things which I have perhaps realized by different means."[169]

What Matisse neglected to say was that there was one major exception to this continuity between the *Bonheur de vivre* and his late works: the *intimiste* paintings that he did in Nice during the 1920s. It was the Barnes murals that allowed him to find his way back from that digression to the main line of his development.

The image of the dance, which Matisse worked with in one way or another throughout much of his career, had also first been used in the *Bonheur de vivre,* and when Matisse worked on the Barnes mural he was intensely aware of this continuity:

> I had conceived this *Danse* long before, and had put it in the *Bonheur de vivre,* then in my first big dance composition [for Shchukin].... I had the surface in my head. But once the drawing was finished, when I came to color it, I had to change all the pre-arranged forms. I had to fill the entire thing and give a whole that would remain architectural. On the other hand I had to stay in strict conjunction with the masonry, so that the lines would hold their own against the enormous, projecting blocks of the downcurving arches, and even more important, so that the lines would move across them with sufficient vitality to harmonize with each other. To compose

with all that and to obtain something alive and singing, I could only proceed by groping my way and continually modifying my compartments of colors and blacks.[170]

Seeing the three large versions of the mural together is an instructive experience. In the *Unfinished Dance Mural* Matisse consciously sought an effect of great monumentality—one might even say, of giganticism. As opposed to the continuous round of dancers that had formed the basis of the dance theme in the *Bonheur de vivre* and the 1909–1910 *Dance* panels, the *Unfinished Dance Mural* emphasizes the separateness of the gesturing figures. The figures in the *Unfinished Dance Mural* have a curious solipsism about them: each dancer is wrapped up in his or her own narcissistic gestures, virtually unconscious of the others.[171] This effect may have been produced in part by Matisse's use of life drawings of the individual figures as the basis for the various parts of the composition. But it is also the product of a very different conception of dance itself.

The 1909 and 1910 versions of *Dance* depict a round of dancers who are connected to each other in a communal activity, as in folkdances. And, in fact, Matisse's main sources for this imagery came from folk and popular dances, such as the sardana and the farandole. The imagery in the Barnes mural, by contrast, is clearly based on modern dance, and it emphasizes its characteristic, highly individualized, and isolated movements.

The Shchukin *Dance* panel had been executed at a time when Matisse was interested in Russian ballet, but before Nijinsky had developed the radically new manner of dancing and choreography that he employed in *Jeux* (1912) and especially in *The Rite of Spring,* first performed in Paris in 1913. In both these ballets the movements were athletic, explosive, and primitivistic. The dancing in *The Rite of Spring* has been characterized as "an attempt to capture in movement the sheer, driving force of nature, irrational and amoral—nature understood as including man."[172] Further, although *The Rite of Spring* was an ensemble ballet, the "ensemble groupings were deployed asymmetrically, their movements 'hatched in isolation,'" and they were characterized as being "'like those spontaneous fires that break out in haystacks'...the choreography consisted largely of shudders, jerks, stamps, and thudding runs."[173]

The dynamic yet isolated gestures of the dancers in the *Unfinished Dance Mural* seem to follow implicitly the aesthetics of modern, rather than traditional, dance (see fig. 54). In this context, it should be noted that Matisse's earliest studies of dancing figures for the murals recall the poses in Rodin's sculptures of Nijinsky and drawings of dancers (see figs. 55–56).

As MATISSE WORKED on the early cut-paper stages of what became the *Paris Dance Mural,* he retained the lateral flow of the figures even as he reduced the ambient space around them. The early stages of the mural composition (figs. 28–30) are striking for the fluidity with which the background forms are handled and for the bold abstraction of the figures. The right-hand fig-

54. Jean Cocteau, poster for Ballets Russes with Nijinsky in Bakst's costume for *Le spectre de la rose,* 1911.

Severin Wunderman Museum, Irvine, California

55. Auguste Rodin, *Dance Movement*, 1911.
31.2 x 20 cm

Musée Rodin, Paris

56. *Untitled (Dancer)*, 1931. Pencil on paper,
32.2 x 25.7 cm

Musée National d'Art Moderne, Centre
Georges Pompidou, Paris

57. *Acrobats*, 1952. Gouache and charcoal
on paper, 213 x 209.5 cm

Private collection

ure in the Barnes Foundation's small gouache (fig. 33), for example, clearly anticipates the abstract renderings of the human body in some of the late cutouts, notably the severely abstracted figures in works like *Acrobats* (fig. 57) and *Women with Monkeys* (fig. 58) of 1952. But it seems that as Matisse progressed, he realized that the fluid forms he was using would work against the architecture rather than in harmony with it. At the time when he discovered that the dimensions were wrong, he was already working toward a conception that placed stronger emphasis on vertical rhythmic divisions.

Around this same time, Matisse also became increasingly concerned with emphasizing the artificiality of the figures he was creating for the mural. His work on the mural led him to formulate a new, conscious attitude toward his imagery, in which he emphasized simplicity and the conception of what he began to call "signs." At the beginning of 1932, when Matisse was questioned about the art of Manet, he emphasized Manet's directness and simplicity. He enunciated, apparently for the first time, an idea that he returned to repeatedly in later years: "A great painter is one who finds personal and lasting signs that express in plastic terms the spirit of his vision."[174]

When Matisse began the *Merion Dance Mural* he reconceived the whole rhythmic nature of his design, which is much more compartmentalized

58. *Women with Monkeys*, 1952. Gouache and charcoal on paper, 71.7 x 286.2 cm

Museum Ludwig, Cologne, Ludwig Collection

than the earlier composition. And once again he projected a different notion of the dance itself. From the beginning this composition was conceived primarily in terms of three pairs of violently interacting (and clearly female) dancers, set in contrast with two recumbent figures. As the composition developed, it became increasingly violent and more explicitly sexual. The final version is a kind of athletic *lutte d'amour* between Amazons.

Curiously enough, as Matisse developed this composition, he reverted to some illusionistic devices, such as foreshortened figures and landscape elements, as if intent on retaining at least a remnant of illusionistic space. If the figures in the *Merion Dance Mural* emanate an impressive monumentality, it is in part because they are rendered in a gigantic decorative way, very much in keeping with the cool sensuality and decorative monumentality common to so much art deco imagery.

This gigantesque aspect of the mural deeply impressed Dorothy Dudley when she saw the *Merion Dance Mural* in Matisse's studio shortly before he took it to Merion. "Eight giant figures against shafts of sky in a tremendous dance of goddesses," she wrote. "The flesh grey between black and white, like the walls of the room in Merion; the sky vivid cobalt blue and brilliant rose, which for a limpid narrow margin around the bodies deepens to a darker blue and rose; the grey of the flesh influenced against the blue toward orange, against the rose toward green."[175]

If the *Merion Dance Mural* falls a bit short of our highest expectations—as it apparently did for Barnes—this is in part because the figures are not quite integrated with the wall. Despite the strong, rhythmic effect of the near vertical blacks that both accent and contain the downward thrusts of the arches, the figures are drawn so that they occupy a fairly illusionistic three-dimensional space. This effect of illusionism is enhanced by surprising passages of modeling, such as in the tumbling lower figure in the central panel, with its intensely modeled abdominal area, and with its vivid use of illusionistic cast shadow.

In this composition the vocabulary of the descriptive forms is somewhat at odds with the spatial indicators. The truncated right arm of that same tumbling figure, for example, is very inventively conceived, but the shadows around it give it a discomfiting literalness and impose an exaggerated stylization upon it. It looks, quite literally, as if it were cut out of paper, but it is too corporeal an image to function as a pictorially independent abstract sign.

WHEN MATISSE RETURNED TO THE FIRST VERSION of the mural in the fall of 1933, it too was still fairly illusionistic, though not nearly as much so as the *Merion Dance Mural*—in large measure because he had not added cast shadows. The transformation of this work between February 1932 and November 1933 is remarkable. Here, in this final version, Matisse was able to resolve many of the formal problems that had plagued him all along. He was at last able to impose a set of rhythms on the figures that seems to come from *outside* their own physical being. This can be clearly seen in the second figure from the right. In the 1932 gouache (fig. 34), and in the contemporaneous in-progress photograph of the mural (fig. 35), that figure seems to tumble behind the pendentive. But in the final version of the *Paris Dance Mural,* the figure in that position is intensely flattened and geometricized; quite literally she becomes an integral part of the structure of the arch that she straddles; her right arm acts as a kind of flying buttress that seems to support the arch, while the rest of her body is spread across the surface of the arch and aligned in such a way as to seem to help support it.

A similar emphasis on the architectonic structure of the figures themselves can be perceived throughout the whole *Paris Dance Mural.* When Matisse first began to rework it in October 1933, he started to make it more like the *Merion Dance Mural,* in which the arabesques of the figures are set in counterpoint to the lunette shapes. But soon after he began the revisions, he decided to return to a flatter, more architectonic, and more abstract conception.

In revising his composition, Matisse also reconceived its emotional expressiveness. The imagery of the final version of the *Paris Dance Mural* is more austere and less physical than the earlier versions of the composition. It is also more architectonic than the *Merion Dance Mural,* and the individual figures in it are less clearly animated. While in the Merion mural the rhythms of the dancing and tumbling figures are set in harmony with the curves of the three-part arcade, in the Paris version the figures move across the surface like participants in a staccato frieze. Although one can still speak of figures and ground in the Paris version of the mural, there is virtually no sense of *fore*ground and *back*ground. The space is unified into a new kind of abstracted entity, which clearly anticipates the ethereal space and abstracted sign language of the late cutouts.

In fact, the pictorial structure of the final version of the *Paris Dance Mural* is much closer to that of the late cutouts than to any of the previous versions of the Barnes mural project. This is because its underlying spatial construction is flatter and more abstract. The figures are less three-dimensional and much more signlike than in the previous versions, and their disposition closely follows the internal structural logic of the three lunette shapes that contain them.

In the *Merion Dance Mural* fairly equal emphasis is given to all eight figures, and there is a direct interaction between the three pairs of dancers. The *Paris Dance Mural,* in contrast, is dominated by figures who seem to be jumping and tumbling almost in isolation from each other. While the *Merion Dance Mural* emphasizes a kind of Dionysian ecstasy, the *Paris Dance Mural* conveys a sense of nervous excitement very much in keeping with what Matisse, while he was working on it, described as its "warrior-like character."[176] This contrast between an aggressive and a lyrical conception of the dance parallels a similar contrast between the two versions of the 1909–1910 *Dance* panels, in which the version now at the Museum of Modern Art is lyrical and ethereal, while the Hermitage Museum version is more aggressive and earthy.

Matisse was fully aware of the different effects produced by his two finished versions of the Barnes mural. In 1934 he wrote to the Russian art critic Alexandre Romm that the two versions of the Barnes mural were quite different:

> The second [Merion version] is not a simple copy of the first: for, because these different pendentives required me to compose with architectural masses more than twice the size, I had to change my composition. I even produced a work with a different spirit: the first [Paris version] is aggressive, the second [Merion version] Dionysiac; the colors, which are the same, are nonetheless changed; the quantities being different, their quality also changes: the colors applied freely show that it is their quantitative relation that produces their quality.[177]

Romm replied that the Merion panel was "a logical follow-up of the Moscow *Dance,*" but said that he felt the human element in it was less pronounced. Matisse, no doubt still smarting from Barnes' recent criticism of his work on these grounds, responded by saying that "the object of the two works was not the same; the problem was different."[178] He explained:

> In architectural painting, which is the case in Merion, it seems to me that the human element has to be tempered, if not excluded. I, who let myself always be guided by my instinct (so much so that it manages to overcome my reason), had to avoid it, for it led me away from my architectural problem each time it appeared on my canvas. The expression of this painting should be associated with the severity of a volume of white-washed stone, and an equally white, bare vault. Further, the spectator should not be arrested by this human character with which he would identify, and which by stopping him there would keep him apart from the great, harmonious, living and animated association of the architecture and the painting.[179]

In an implicit defense of the plastic values that Barnes had criticized, Matisse went on to pose a rhetorical question:

> Didn't Raphael and Michelangelo, despite the abstraction resulting from all the richness of mind that they expended on their murals, weigh down their walls with the expression of this humanity, which constantly separates us from the ensemble, notably in the *Last Judgment*? This human sentiment is possible in an easel picture—an easel picture is like a book—its interest does not overwhelm the spectator who must stand in front of it; the place

it will hang is not fixed in advance. It can change places without essentially modifying its place. The painter, then, has more freedom to enrich it.[180]

Matisse's disavowal of the desirability of the "expression of humanity" in the mural has been interpreted as indicative of his "highly restrictive view of the tasks of representation that figurative modernism might perform."[181] It seems, however, that Matisse's suppression of the "human element" here is specifically related to his ambitions for mural painting per se. At this time, Matisse was preoccupied with the potentialities of a public art—especially after having spent most of the 1920s painting intimate pictures. "Architectural painting depends absolutely on the place that has to receive it," Matisse told Romm, "and which it animates with a new life. Once it is placed there, it cannot be separated. It...encloses the spectator in a feeling of release. In this case, it is the spectator who becomes the human element of the work.... I congratulate the directors of the Russian B.[eaux] A.[rts] on their excellent idea to have public monuments decorated by their painters; that is where the great problem is, at present."[182]

While he was working on the Merion mural, Matisse had engaged in long conversations about mural painting with André Masson and had waxed enthusiastic on the subject. "If I were given a great wall to decorate," he told André Gide, "I'd be content to live on dry bread and water."[183] Throughout most of his career Matisse was preoccupied with what might be called a private art. His enthusiasm for mural painting in the early 1930s reflects his desire for a different sort of art, one that would be monumental and public. Such an art might release him from the sense of spiritual isolation that he felt at the time, by playing a role within a broader social context—for the artist as well as for the public. In 1929 he had told Florent Fels that he believed in "the possibility of an art pursued in common," and in 1931 Christian Zervos reported that Matisse "dreamt of turning painting into a collective activity."[184]

Such an art, moreover, had a certain inherent heroism about it. "A painter who composes on the grand scale," Matisse said to Louis Aragon in 1942, "carried away by the movement of his picture, cannot stop over details." This procedure of generalization was one that Matisse aspired to in much of his late work, in which his pictorial language became increasingly abstract and signlike. He felt, he told Aragon, as if he were going to take on large-scale compositions: "It's odd, isn't it? As if I had all my life ahead of me, or rather a whole other life... I don't know, but the quest for signs—I felt absolutely obliged to go on searching for signs in preparation for a new development in my life as a painter... Perhaps after all I have an unconscious belief in a future life... some paradise where I shall paint frescoes."[185]

The simplicity of the figures and the extreme flattening of the space in the *Paris Dance Mural* had significant repercussions in Matisse's later work. The space in the mural functions not only as a *pictorial* space but also, for the first time, as a *real* wall space within an architectural ensemble. This space and the signlike pictorial language that Matisse created for it were quite different from anything he had done earlier. They are anticipated indirectly only by a few previous works, such as the 1916 *Moroccans* and *Bathers by a River,* both of which employ a similarly abstracted and sectioned-off spatial construction.[186]

Matisse had the *Paris Dance Mural* in his studio until just before he began his first independent works in cut and pasted paper.[187] The imagery of some of the earlier cutouts is quite descriptive, as in *Two Dancers* of 1938. But eventually the cutouts provided him with a medium in which he could achieve an art based on abstract signs set in an abstracted, disembodied space, as in the illustrations for *Jazz.* The *Paris Dance Mural* seems to have played a pivotal role in this development. It anticipates the increasingly abstracted imagery of the late cutouts, and it also served as an opening to the large-scale and intense decorative ambition of the mural-like late cutouts, such as *The Parakeet and the Mermaid.* It is in works such as this one that Matisse came closest, in this world at least, to evoking the image of "some paradise where I shall paint frescoes."

MATISSE'S WORK ON THE MURAL PROJECT in general precipitated important changes in his working procedures. Although in the past he had sometimes photographed his works while they were in progress, with the Barnes murals he did this more systematically than ever before. He frequently employed this practice later, and it reflects a new self-consciousness about the act of creation. This is also reflected in the numerous drawings he did later in the decade, which depict him in the act of creating the picture we are looking at.[188]

The Barnes project also involved the development of the technical device of using large sheets of painted paper to try out compositional changes without having to do extensive repainting. Matisse used this device increasingly during the mid-1930s, in paintings like *Large Reclining Nude (Pink Nude).*[189] He used cut and pasted paper—and the architectural setting of the Barnes mural—again a few years later, when he designed the decor for Massine's ballet *Rouge et noir* (1937–1938), which was first performed in Monte Carlo in 1939 (fig. 59). In the late 1930s he began to use cut and pasted paper as the basis for magazine cover designs, and over the years he repeatedly returned to images of dancers when called on to do small decorative commissions, such as the 1945 cover for *Verve.* Eventually he came to use the paper cutout as a medium in itself. Although Matisse had used cut and pasted paper as a compositional aid as far back as 1920, when he worked on the costume designs for the ballet *Le chant du rossignol,* he had used the medium then on a much smaller scale and in a very different way: purely for decorative effect. In the Barnes murals, by contrast, he used cut paper to generate representational imagery on a large scale.

The Barnes murals were an important transitional stage in the develop-

59. Performance of the ballet *Rouge et noir*, 1939
Private collection

ment of the cutout technique. The cut-paper technique that Matisse employed in the compositions for the murals was different from that of the later cutouts. For the mural compositions he used small pieces of paper in a cumulative way, almost as equivalents of the brushstrokes in painting. In the later cutouts he no longer built up his images out of small pieces of paper. Instead he cut bold, signlike forms directly out of large swaths of brightly colored paper. Among the ground-breaking innovations associated with the Barnes murals, one must count Matisse's earliest extensive use of cut and pinned paper and also the conceptual basis for the new signlike pictorial language that characterized the late cutouts.

More immediately, Matisse's experience with the Barnes murals contributed to the radical change in his painting in the 1930s, as he worked toward a new balance between drawing and color. During the summer of 1935 he wrote to his son Pierre that he was involved in "un travail de recherches." He felt that his recent, brightly colored paintings were the beginning of a new way of working, which would allow for a greater synthesis between color and line.[190]

The Barnes murals were especially important because they brought Matisse back to his crucial notion of the importance of emphasizing the purity of his means of expression, a return to essentials. In 1936, when his painting was in the midst of the radical transformation initiated by the Barnes mural project, he affirmed that he had at last come full circle. In a declaration to Tériade that reads like a manifesto, he said:

> When the means of expression have become so refined, so attenuated that their power of expression wears thin, it is necessary to return to the essential principles which made human language. They are, after all, the principles which "go back to the source," which relive, which give us life. Pictures which have become refinements, subtle gradations, dissolutions without energy, call for beautiful blues, reds, yellows—matter to stir the sensual depths in men. This is the starting point of Fauvism: the courage to return to the purity of the means.[191]

To which he added: "In my latest paintings, I have united the acquisitions of the last twenty years to my essential core, to my very essence."

It was the Barnes mural project that opened the way for Matisse's return to the most essential sources of his art. ◾

1. This set of large canvases was found after the death of the artist's son, Pierre Matisse, in the course of settling his estate. The discovery was first reported by Pierre Schneider, "Henri Matisse: 'La Danse' ressuscitée," *L'Express,* 28 May 1992, 156–162.

2. Sergei Shchukin signed his letters to Matisse "Stschoukine," but since the former spelling has now become familiar in English and better conforms to English-language conventions for transliterating Russian names, I retain it here.

3. Henri Matisse to Pierre Matisse, 1 January 1927, Pierre Matisse Archives. See Jack Cowart et al., *Matisse and Morocco* [exh. cat., National Gallery of Art] (Washington, 1990).

4. E. Tériade, "Visite à Henri Matisse," *L'Intransigeant,* 14 and 22 January 1929; English translation in Jack D. Flam, *Matisse on Art* (London, 1973), 59. Here, as elsewhere, I have sometimes modified my earlier translations in the interest of clarity.

5. Tériade 1929; trans. Flam 1973, 58.

6. Florent Fels, *Henri-Matisse* (Paris, 1929), 50.

7. For Lisette Carnète's reminiscences of the time she spent with Matisse, see C. de Peslöuan, "Matisse photographe," *Jours de France Madame,* 27 November 1989, 39–41.

8. For color reproductions of these paintings, see Jack Cowart and Dominique Fourcade, *Henri Matisse: The Early Years in Nice, 1916–1930* [exh. cat., National Gallery of Art] (Washington, 1986), 230, 232.

9. E. Tériade, "L'actualité de Matisse," *Cahiers d'art* 4(7) (1929), 286.

10. Fritz Neugass, "Henri Matisse: Pour son soixantième anniversaire," *Cahier de Belgique* 3 (March 1930), 100; English translation in Jack Flam, *Matisse: A Retrospective* (New York, 1988), 244. The exhibition at the Berlin gallery ran from 15 February to 19 March 1930.

11. André Levinson, "Les soixante ans de Henri Matisse," *L'Art vivant* 6(121) (January 1930), 27; trans. Flam 1988, 243.

12. Levinson 1930, 27; trans. Flam 1988, 243–244.

13. Pierre Schneider, *Matisse* (New York, 1984), 606–607.

14. Matisse discussed his trips to Tahiti and New York in an interview with E. Tériade, "Entretien avec Tériade," *L'Intransigeant,* 20 and 27 October 1930; trans. Flam 1973, 60–64. One cannot help but wonder whether the "gold nugget" image reflected some of his expectations regarding the legendary wealth of American collectors.

15. Henri Matisse to Pierre Matisse, Papeete, 6 June 1930, Pierre Matisse Archives, New York.

16. Tériade 1930; trans. Flam 1973, 61.

17. Matisse had been commissioned by Skira early in 1930, and the book was published on 25 October 1932. The actual contract seems to have been confirmed in April, in Matisse's absence. See Claude Duthuit, *Henri Matisse: Catalogue raisonné des ouvrages illustrés établi avec la collaboration de Françoise Garnaud* (Paris, 1988), 16–17.

18. Matisse mentioned his attempt to rework *The Yellow Dress* in his interview with Tériade. See Tériade 1930; trans. Flam 1973, 60.

19. On 10 August 1930, Guillaume Lerolle, the European representative of the

Carnegie Institute, sent Marguerite Duthuit, Matisse's daughter, a copy of her father's projected itinerary. He was to arrive in New York on 19 September and spend three days there; he would then spend two days in Pittsburgh, two days in Washington, and one day in Philadelphia, before returning to New York for three or four days and leaving for France on 1 October (Matisse Archives, Paris). Matisse seems to have extended the time of his stay a few days, at his own expense, in order to follow up on Dr. Barnes' proposal for the mural.

20. Barnes to Matisse, (21?) September 1930, Barnes Foundation Archives, Merion, Pennsylvania. It has been said that Barnes tried to persuade Matisse to come to Merion instead of going to Pittsburgh; see William Schack, *Art and Argyrol* (New York, 1960), 223–224. But I have found no evidence for this assertion.

21. In the 1926 Barnes Foundation inventory, twenty-three Matisses were already listed. Many more had been added later, and in 1930 Barnes was still very actively collecting Matisse.

22. Matisse wrote this phrase, then crossed it out, in a brief text about the mural in one of his notebooks, known as "Repertoire 6," written around 1946. This notebook also contains a draft for some of the text of Matisse's illustrated book *Jazz,* published in 1947. Parts of this text are given in Schneider 1984, 622. My thanks to Pierre Schneider for allowing me to see a copy of the original handwritten text.

23. See Schack 1963, 223–225; also Howard Greenfeld, *The Devil and Dr. Barnes: Portrait of an American Art Collector* (New York, 1987), 159–161.

24. Matisse agenda (pocket diary), 27 September 1930, Matisse Archives.

25. An exchange of messages in the Barnes Foundation Archives reveals that Matisse contacted Barnes the very next day (28 September) to fix the date for a second visit.

26. Matisse's agenda notes that he had written to Barnes the day after his return to Paris, on 11 October 1930, but this letter has been lost.

27. The plaster *Back* was at that time stored in his studio at Issy-les-Moulineaux, a suburb of Paris. Matisse had evidently begun the fourth *Back* while he was in Paris during the month of August 1929, and in his agenda for 28 October 1930 he listed the four works as follows: "Bas Relief 1er état 1909/2ème état 1912/3ème état..../4ème état 1930."

28. Tériade 1930; trans. Flam 1973, 63. Matisse was actually interviewed by Tériade over a period of three days: 15, 17, and 22 October (Matisse agenda).

29. Tériade 1930; trans. Flam 1973, 60.

30. "Carnegie Show," *Time,* 20 October 1930. A similar point was also made in an interview published in *The Literary Digest,* 18 October 1930, 21–22.

31. In 1934 Matisse told Dorothy Dudley that he had been misquoted about American artists traveling: "Very likely your artists would need to go to Paris as a mere matter of education. But they wrote down that Matisse believed the American should stay home! Why did they do that?" Dorothy Dudley, "The Matisse Fresco in Merion, Pennsylvania," *Hound & Horn* 7(2) (January–March 1934), 301–302. Matisse discussed these issues in a conversation with the American painter George L. K. Morris, whom he met on the train from Cherbourg to Paris. According to Morris, Matisse said that American artists should stay home, but Morris was aware of a certain irony in Matisse's remarks. The account from Morris' diary was published as "A Brief Encounter with Matisse," *Life,* 28 August 1970, 44.

32. Barnes' stay in Paris is alluded to in a letter of 4 May 1931, which mentions his earlier stay at the Hotel Mirabeau (Barnes Foundation Archives). On 16 November 1930 Marguerite Duthuit wrote to Etta Cone in Baltimore saying that her father had just accepted a commission to make a large decoration for the Barnes Foundation (Cone Archives, Baltimore Museum of Art).

33. For the chronology of the Cones' acquisitions, see Brenda Richardson, *Dr. Claribel and Miss Etta: The Cone Collection* [exh. cat., Baltimore Museum of Art] (Baltimore, 1985), 163–194.

34. The date of the commission is usually given as January 1931. See Alfred H. Barr, Jr., *Matisse: His Art and His Public* (New York, 1951), 220; and Washington 1986, 39. The actual letter of agreement, which was written in both French and English, is dated 20 December 1930 (Barnes Foundation Archives). The French version stipulates: "Nous devons vous payer dix mille ($10.000) dollars au début du travail, un deuxième paiement de dix mille ($10.000) dollars lorsque le travail sera à moitié terminé, et un troisième paiement de dix mille ($10.000) dollars lorsque les peintures seront installeés dans notre galerie. Il est entendu qu'il vous faudra environ une anneé pour terminer le travail."

35. Matisse to Amélie Matisse, 22 December 1930, Matisse Archives.

36. "Each was the first person the other had ever met with a will as strong as his own, but in spite of or perhaps in consequence of this, they seemed to have a great respect and even a certain fascination for each other" (Jane Simon Bussy, "A Great Man," *The Burlington Magazine* 128[995] [February 1986], 82).

37. Barnes to John Dewey, 2 January 1931, Barnes Foundation Archives.

38. Matisse to Amélie Matisse, 22 December 1930, Matisse Archives. Matisse's agenda entries note some of his conversations with Barnes.

39. The most detailed account of the relationship between Matisse and Shchukin is given in Albert Kostenevich and Natalya Semyonova, *Collecting Matisse: The Early Years in Russia* (Paris, 1992).

40. Matisse wrote to his wife that the template was difficult to make because the wall and the ceiling were round. "Tout va bien. C'est à dire que Barnes est content, qu'on travaille pour relever le gabarit du panneau et du plafond ce qui n'est pas facile parce qu'il est rond. J'ai fait le noël à Merion. Je viens d'en revenir, c'est à dire que j'ai dîné avec M & MMe tout simplement. Et que j'ai travaillé au gabarit" (Matisse to Amélie Matisse, 26 December 1930, Matisse Archives).

41. Matisse to Amélie Matisse, 26 December 1930, Matisse Archives.

42. In October 1930 Matisse told Tériade that he planned to finish *The Yellow Dress* when he returned to Nice; he returned in mid-January (Tériade 1930; trans. Flam 1973, 60).

43. This building is often described as a film studio, but when Edward Dreibelbies visited Matisse there in August 1931, he described it clearly as a garage (Dreibelbies to Barnes, 2 August 1931, Barnes Foundation Archives). See Washington 1986, 39–42, for photographs of the building and a discussion of its function.

44. Dreibelbies to Barnes, 2 August 1931, Barnes Foundation Archives.

45. "Barnes oublie peut être qu'il a dit: la condition principale est que vous la ferez *comme pour vous*" (Matisse to Pierre Matisse, 27 February 1933, Matisse Archives). Matisse repeated this in an interview with Dorothy Dudley: "Besides, he left me free to do what I wanted. He said, 'Paint whatever you like just as if you were painting for yourself'," (Dudley 1934, 301).

46. For analogies between the two works, see Barr 1951, 244–246; Schneider 1984, 605–623. On 5 November 1932 Matisse wrote to his son Pierre that since 20 October he had been working on the decoration and that he had derived "great benefits" from the Mallarmé project (Pierre Matisse Archives).

47. Georges Charbonnier, "Entretien avec Henri Matisse," in *Le monologue du peintre*, vol. 2 (Paris, 1960); trans. Flam 1973, 38. This interview was recorded on tape in August 1950 and broadcast in January 1951.

48. Charbonnier 1960; trans. Flam 1973, 138–139.

49. Friedrich Nietzsche, *The Birth of Tragedy* (1872); English translation in Clifton P. Fadiman, *The Philosophy of Nietzsche* (New York, 1954), 653. See also the interesting discussions of Nietzsche in Albert Kostenevich, "*La Danse* and *La Musique* by Henri Matisse: A New Interpretation," *Apollo* (December 1974), 504–513; and Schneider 1984, 290–294. What were perceived as the Nietzschean aspects of Matisse's art were also

discussed by the American aesthetician Matthew Stewart Prichard and the French philosopher Camille Schuwer, who in 1910 wrote a lengthy analysis of *Dance* in relation to Nietzsche's philosophy.

50. In 1907 Matisse's friend Guillaume Apollinaire published an essay, "La danse est un sport," in a sports magazine (*La culture physique* 50 [1 February 1907]). For Apollinaire's views on the relationship between dance and sports, see Pierre Caizergues, *Apollinaire journaliste: Textes retrouvés et textes inédits avec présentation et notes,* vol. 3 [dissertation, University of Paris III, 1977] (Lille, 1979), 243–245. On the relationship between dance and sport, see also Schneider 1984, 294.

51. Schneider 1984, 626.

52. "Dis à Lisette de faire ce qu'il faut pour être en forme gymnastique, car je vais avoir besoin d'elle" (Matisse to Amélie Matisse, 31 December 1930, Matisse Archives).

53. Pesloüan 1989, 43.

54. "Matisse Speaks," *Art News* 31 (3 June 1933), 8. For an interesting discussion of Matisse in relation to social issues, see John O'Brian, *Ruthless Hedonism: The Reception of Matisse in America, 1929–1954* [dissertation, Harvard University, 1990] (Ann Arbor, 1991), 120–132.

55. Barr 1951, 220–221.

56. Matisse sent the photographs to his wife in a letter dated 31 December 1930 (Matisse Archives). The tracings that Matisse probably gave to Barnes in 1930 appear to have been taken from drawings now in the Musée Matisse, Nice (see *Henri Matisse Dessins: Collection du Musée Matisse* [Nice, 1988], nos. 95, 96). These tracings were sold at auction by the Violette de Mazia Collection in 1989, misdated 1931–1932. See Christie's, *Impressionist and Modern Drawings and Watercolors, Thursday, May 11, 1989* (New York, 1989), nos. 164, 165.

57. This desire to have a more accommodating surface, I believe, must have contributed to his misuse of the template that had been made of the wall. I do not mean to say, of course, that Matisse's misuse of the template was willful, but rather that he was disinclined to question the discrepancy of measurements when he should have, because the lunettes with the narrow pendentives offered a better potential format for his painting.

58. "I had conceived this *Danse* long before," Matisse later told an interviewer, "and had put it in the *Bonheur de vivre,* then in my first big dance composition [for Shchukin]. This time however when I wanted to make sketches on three canvases one meter long, I couldn't get it. Finally I took three canvases of five meters each, the actual dimensions of the panels, and one day, armed with charcoal on the end of a bamboo stick, I set out to draw the whole thing at one go. It was in me like a rhythm that carried me along" (Gaston Diehl, interview with Matisse, *Les arts et les lettres* [April 1946]; trans. Flam 1973, 173 n.6). What Matisse neglects to say in the later account is that the first drawings on the full-size canvases were not freely rendered but followed the small sketches very closely. The large drawing of the central dancer may have been one of several large drawings that were used to make a cartoon.

59. This undated letter seems to be one of at least two drafts for Matisse's 24 April 1931 letter to Barnes; it can be dated by internal evidence to early April 1931 and seems in any event to have been written before 10 April, when Matisse sent his daughter Marguerite another draft of the 24 April letter (Matisse Archives). The care that Matisse took in composing such letters reveals his anxiety about his dealings with Barnes. He had been similarly careful in his dealings with Shchukin some twenty years earlier.

60. This is apparent in a draft of a letter to Barnes (the final letter was sent on 24 April) that Matisse sent to his daughter Marguerite on 10 April 1931. In this draft he wrote: "La voussure dessinée au dessus des panneaux est provisoire celles qui seront posées définitivement chez vous seront peintes par morceaux dans les vides qui sont dans les toiles au dessus et autour des arceaux en X sur le croquis ci-contre." In the April 24th letter, Matisse did not include the sketch referred to in the draft. But the painting-in of the

areas around the picture is indicated in a sketch included in Matisse's letter to Barnes of 15 May, and remnants of the plan can be seen in the borders of the *Unfinished Dance Mural.*

61.   On the likely use of a cartoon for the final version of the Shchukin *Dance,* see Flam 1986, 495 n.41.

62.   "Serie I—Premier contact avec la surface. Serie II—deuxième attaque, plus architecturale je crois—Je suis en ce moment aux recherches de couleurs" (Matisse to Barnes, 24 April 1931, Barnes Foundation Archives).

63.   Matisse pursued this as a conscious goal. In the draft letter he sent to his daughter on 10 April, he wrote that in the second series of photographs, "je pense que le dessin est plus large et davantage destiné à être complété par les couleurs" (Matisse Archives).

64.   Matisse Archives.

65.   Barnes to Matisse, 5 May 1931, Barnes Foundation Archives.

66.   Matisse to Barnes, 15 May 1931, Barnes Foundation Archives.

67.   Barnes Foundation checkbook, 16 June 1931, Barnes Foundation Archives. Barnes had originally hoped to see the mural in progress when he came to France in June. On 10 February 1931, he had written Matisse saying, "I suppose you have begun the paintings for the Foundation. How I would like to see you at work on these canvases, and how much I want to have them in our gallery! I am certain that you will accomplish a work worthy of your great talent and of the Foundation. Perhaps when I am in France in June you will let me see what you have done" (Barnes Foundation Archives). The Georges Petit exhibition was Matisse's first Parisian retrospective since 1910.

68.   Barnes to John Dewey, 6 November 1931, Barnes Foundation Archives.

69.   This story was recounted by Violette de Mazia, who accompanied Barnes to Paris. My thanks to Nicolas King for relating this to me.

70.   Dreibelbies to Barnes, 2 August 1931. The canvases were eventually mounted on wooden stretchers.

71.   Henry Hart, *Dr. Barnes of Merion* (New York, 1963), 81.

72.   Matisse to Bonnard, 7 May 1946, in "Correspondance Matisse-Bonnard," *La nouvelle revue française* 18 (212) (August 1970), 70.

73.   Matisse went to Padua on 12 September 1931 (Matisse agenda). While in Italy he also traveled to Milan to see Leonardo da Vinci's *Last Supper.*

74.   Matisse had clearly not begun to work with cut paper when Dreibelbies visited him in August; he began to do so after his return from Italy.

75.   This account of Matisse's technique is taken from my interview with Lydia Delectorskaya (Paris, 12 June 1992), who worked as Matisse's assistant on the Merion mural in 1932–1933, and from the published account by Lisette Clarnète as given in interviews with C. de Peslöuan, published in Pesloüan 1989.

76.   Bussy 1986, 82.

77.   Charbonnier 1960; trans. Flam 1973, 139.

78.   Matisse, letter to Alexandre Romm, 19 January 1934; trans. Flam 1973, 68.

79.   Dudley 1934, 299.

80.   Charbonnier 1960; trans. Flam 1973, 139.

81.   See André Verdet, *Prestiges de Matisse* (Paris, 1952); trans. Flam 1973, 144. Although the doors proper had transparent panes, they were covered with nearly opaque curtains. My thanks to Nicolas King for pointing out to me that the doors would have been opened at the time of Matisse's first visit.

82.   Matisse, "Repertoire 6," c. 1946. The bracketed words "unfavorable" and "not being very favorable" are crossed out in the manuscript. Matisse also includes a sketch of the wall. Part of this text is given by Schneider 1984, 622, but it is abridged without the elisions being indicated.

83.   Barnes to Matisse, 21 October 1931, Barnes Foundation Archives.

84. Matisse to Barnes, 6 November 1931, Barnes Foundation Archives.

85. Matisse to Pierre Matisse, 29 November 1931, Pierre Matisse Archives.

86. "Matisse Finishing Mural for America," *New York Times,* 9 February 1932.

87. In a letter of 26 December 1930 to his wife, Matisse mentioned that he helped work on a template that was being made for "the panel and the ceiling which is not easy because it is round" (Matisse Archives).

88. Matisse wrote Barnes on 16 January 1931 saying that he had "the precious template package" with him. On 9 March 1931 Matisse cabled Barnes: "AI OUBLIE PLAN MUR EN PAPIER BLEU PRIERE ENVOYER—STOP. TRAVAIL MARCHE" (Matisse Archives). Barnes replied the next day: "PAPIER BLEU ENVOIE *[sic]*" (Barnes Foundation Archives).

89. Matisse to Barnes, 2 February 1932, Matisse Archives.

90. Barnes to Matisse, 2 February 1932, Matisse Archives.

91. These cables and Barnes' letter of 2 February 1932 are in the Matisse Archives. The French text of Barnes' 22 February cable is as follows: "AVEZ FAIT ERREUR ENORME STOP DIMENSIONS REELLES BASE PENDENTIF GAUCHE UN METRE BASE PENDENTIF DROIT UN METRE ONZE MILLIMETRES STOP GABARIT NOUS VOUS AVIONS DONN[E] AVAIT DIMENSIONS CORRECTES STOP VOTRE ERREUR RESULTE VOTRE OMISSION BANDE QUARANTE CINQ CENTIMETRES BASE PEND[E]NTIF GAUCHE ET BANDE QUARANTE CINQ CENTIMETRES SEPT MILLIMETRES BASE PENDENTIF DROIT LESQUELLES BANDES ETAIENT INCLU[S]ES DANS PAQUET GABARIT VOUS AVIEZ STOP DOIS-JE VENIR PARIS IMMEDIATEMENT AVEC GABARIT."

92. The text of the telegram is published in Hart 1963, 120. The original French reads: "MILLE EXCUSES COMME NOUVELLE COMPOSITION EST NECESSAIRE JE TERMINE PANNEAUX ACTUELS PRESQUE FINIS ET RECOMMENCE SUR NOUVELLES TOILES ENVOYEZ GABARIT INUTILE VENIR MERCI LETTRE SUIT." I have not been able to locate a copy of the actual telegram, either in the Barnes Foundation Archives or in the Matisse Archives. Hart must have gotten the text from Laura Barnes.

93. Barnes to Keller, 22 February 1932, Barnes Foundation Archives. The picture, however, remained unfinished at this time and was not exhibited at the Galeries Georges Petit.

94. Keller to Barnes, 22 February 1932, Barnes Foundation Archives.

95. Barnes and Matisse met in Paris on 4 March 1932. At this time Barnes had still not seen the mural. (Some twenty-three years earlier, as a similar gesture, Matisse had sent Sergei Shchukin a watercolor of his composition for the *Dance* mural that Shchukin was commissioning from him.) Pierre Matisse saw this gouache when he dined with Barnes in Merion in mid-April (Pierre Matisse to Matisse, 19 April 1932, Pierre Matisse Archives).

96. Pierre Matisse to his parents, 26 February 1932, Pierre Matisse Archives.

97. Pierre Matisse to his parents, 3 March 1932, Pierre Matisse Archives. As can be seen from Pierre's remarks, Matisse and his son had come to realize what a good deal Barnes had struck back in December 1930. Although at the time Matisse had thought that $30,000 was a handsome price for the work required, he later came to realize that Barnes had gotten a bargain. As a point of comparison, at the beginning of 1931 Barnes had paid the substantial price of $15,000 when he bought from Valentine Dudensing the center panel of Matisse's much smaller *Three Sisters* triptych of 1917.

98. Barnes to Matisse, from Bride-les-Bains, 1 July 1932, Matisse Archives.

99. The earlier photographs may have been taken for the express purpose of serving as the basis of the small gouaches Matisse did of the earlier versions (figs. 32–35). For earlier works photographed while in progress, see Flam 1986, 229–231, 366, 417.

100. Raymond Escholier, *Henri Matisse* (Paris, 1937), 141.

101. See Pesloüan 1989, 43. Lisette continued to live with the Matisses, however, until she was asked to leave the following summer. Lisette's departure is mentioned in a letter from Matisse to his son Pierre, 8 August 1933 (Pierre Matisse Archives).

102. See Lydia Delectorskaya, *Henri Matisse, Peintures de 1935–1939...l'apparente facilité...* (Paris, 1986), 14; English translation published as *With Apparent Ease... Henri Matisse* (Paris, 1988).

103. Matisse to Pierre Matisse, 5 November 1932, Pierre Matisse Archives. Here as elsewhere, Matisse refers to the *Merion Dance Mural* as the "second" one and to the *Paris Dance Mural* as the "first."

104. Matisse to Pierre Matisse, 29 November 1932, Pierre Matisse Archives.

105. Pierre Matisse to his parents, 29 November 1932, Pierre Matisse Archives.

106. See John Elderfield, *Henri Matisse: A Retrospective* (New York, 1992), 411, where it is dated 1935–c. 1942. For related drawings, see Schneider 1984, 258.

107. Barnes to Matisse, aboard the *Europa,* 31 December 1932, Matisse Archives.

108. Matisse to Pierre Matisse, from the Hotel Catalonia in Palma de Mallorca, 15 January 1933, Pierre Matisse Archives. Matisse's description of the trip to Mallorca is given in a letter written to Pierre on 2 February 1933, also in the Pierre Matisse Archives.

109. The photographs sent to Barnes range in date from 20 August 1932 to 26 January 1933. Three further photographs were published in *Cahiers d'Art* 10 (1) (1935) and reprinted in Barr 1951, 464; the last of these is dated 7 April 1933. The state in which Barnes saw the mural is almost certainly State XXV, photographed on 26 January while Barnes was still in Nice. This is the last state in the series of photographs presently in the Barnes Foundation Archives; presumably Matisse gave Barnes a complete, or nearly complete, set of photographs while the latter was in Nice.

110. At the beginning of February, he thought he would finish in "a few days" (Matisse to Pierre Matisse, 2 February 1933). At this time Barnes also bought a painting of a nude from Matisse for 50,000 francs.

111. Matisse to Pierre Matisse, 2 February 1933, Pierre Matisse Archives.

112. This state (State XXV) may actually reflect Matisse's work on the composition while Barnes was still in Nice.

113. Delectorskaya interview, 12 June 1992.

114. Matisse to Pierre Matisse, 12 February 1933, Pierre Matisse Archives.

115. Matisse agenda, 21 February 1933.

116. Matisse agenda, 24 February 1933.

117. Matisse to Pierre Matisse, 27 February 1933, Pierre Matisse Archives.

118. Delectorskaya interview, 12 June 1992.

119. Matisse to Simon Bussy, 7 March 1933.

120. Matisse to Pierre Matisse, 13 March 1933, Pierre Matisse Archives.

121. Matisse agenda.

122. Matisse to Marguerite Duthuit, 30 March 1933, Matisse Archives, Paris.

123. Matisse to Marguerite Duthuit, 30 March 1933.

124. Delectorskaya interview, 12 June 1992.

125. "COUPEZ PAS DECORATION APPORTEZ EN UNE PIECE." This is recounted in a letter from Matisse to Pierre Matisse, 23 April 1933, Pierre Matisse Archives.

126. Letter of agreement between the Barnes Foundation and Matisse, 20 December 1930, Barnes Foundation Archives.

127. Matisse to Pierre Matisse, 23 April 1933, Pierre Matisse Archives.

128. Recounted in a letter from Matisse to Pierre Matisse, 23 April 1933, Pierre Matisse Archives.

129. Matisse to Pierre Matisse, 24 April 1933, Pierre Matisse Archives.

130.   Barnes received a cable from Matisse on 3 May 1933, informing him that he was arriving with the large crates and that Barnes should arrange for customs clearance and transport to Merion (Barnes to Pierre Matisse, 3 May 1933). That same day Barnes also wrote to his shippers, Keer, Maurer Company in Philadelphia, to inform them that Matisse was "bringing with him the mural paintings which he did for us. These paintings are enormous, a width of practically fifty (50) feet, and the packing of them is very complicated." Barnes instructed them to meet the boat and have the paintings shipped to Merion in bond, so that the crate would not have to be opened at the Custom House (Pierre Matisse Archives).

131.   Matisse expressed especially harsh judgments about Barnes in letters written to his wife and daughter in May 1933 (Matisse Archives).

132.   Matisse to Marguerite Duthuit, 30 May 1933. Matisse remembered the review as being in *The Burlington Magazine*.

133.   Matisse to Pierre Matisse, 8 February 1934, Pierre Matisse Archives.

134.   Alfred H. Barr, Jr., *Henri-Matisse Retrospective Exhibition* [exh. cat., Museum of Modern Art] (New York, 1931), 22.

135.   Dudley 1934, 300. Dudley interviewed Matisse shortly before he left for Merion with the mural and again shortly after the mural was installed. At present the glass panes are not transparent, and the garden cannot be seen through them.

136.   Barnes to Pierre Matisse, 15 May 1933, Pierre Matisse Archives.

137.   Barnes to Pierre Matisse, 15 May 1933.

138.   Matisse described the installation process in a letter to his wife, but he took care not to alarm her about his health (Matisse to Amélie Matisse, New York, 17 May 1933). The account of Barnes' lecture is given in an undated letter to his daughter Marguerite, written during his return voyage, from Gibraltar, probably on 30 May 1933 (Matisse Archives).

139.   Barnes to Pierre Matisse, 15 May 1933.

140.   Matisse to Amélie Matisse, New York, 17 May 1933.

141.   Matisse to Simon Bussy, from New York, 17 May 1933.

142.   Dudley 1934, 298–303. It is worth noting that in the architect's plans for the building a rosette-like medallion was designed for the center of the middle lunette; it apparently was to have been made of ceramic tile but was not constructed. In comparing the mural to a stained glass window, Barnes may have had this form in mind. On 3 February 1934 Matisse wrote to Barnes asking how the canvases had fared physically during the extreme change of climate during the summer months, and what effect his mural had had on "the spiritual life of the Foundation." On the second matter he had been somewhat assured by a card he had received from Barnes. In the same letter Matisse speaks of having reworked the first version of the mural and of other recent paintings (Barnes Foundation Archives).

143.   On Thursday, 18 May, Matisse sent Barnes a telegram from New York, informing him that "SAUF VOTRE AVIS CONTRAIRE NOUS ARRETERONS AVEC PIERRE FOUNDATION DEMAIN VENDREDI DE UNE A TROIS HEURES AURONS DEJEUNE" (Pierre Matisse Archives). Whether Matisse changed his mind, or whether Barnes asked him not to come, is not known.

144.   Matisse discussed his reactions to Barnes in letters written to his wife and daughter in May 1933 (Matisse Archives).

145.   Pierre Matisse to Matisse, undated letter (February 1934), Pierre Matisse Archives. The day Matisse returned to New York from Merion, he wrote to his wife that "Barnes doesn't want to show it to anybody" (Matisse to Amélie Matisse, 17 May 1933).

146.   Hart 1963, 120. Hart got his information from Laura Barnes, who presumably was privy to her husband's thoughts on the matter.

147.   He did, however, continue to buy, though on a very reduced scale. In the fall of 1936 Barnes told a reporter that he had just bought four recent Matisse interiors: "It's

an amazing thing about Matisse. He's getting on in years, you know, and everyone thought he had shot his bolt in art. He's 67 or 68 years old and he hadn't shown anything in two years. But this year he had a show in Paris that would knock your eye out" (*Time,* 14 September 1936, 69).

148.   Albert C. Barnes and Violette de Mazia, *The Art of Henri Matisse* (New York, 1933), 202–203.

149.   Barnes and de Mazia 1933, 202.

150.   Dudley 1934, 300.

151.   "Matisse Speaks," *Art News* 31 (3 June 1933), 8. This interview was given a few hours before Matisse boarded the *Comté de Savoie* and sailed to France.

152.   Barnes to Matisse, 17 January 1934, Matisse Archives. The effect of this letter was important enough for Matisse to give a detailed account of it in a letter to Pierre Matisse, 8 February 1934 (Pierre Matisse Archives).

153.   Matisse to Barnes, 3 February 1934, Barnes Foundation Archives.

154.   Matisse to Simon Bussy, 18 June 1933.

155.   Etta Cone to Fred Cone, from Nice, 22 July 1933, as cited in Barbara Pollack, *The Collectors: Dr. Claribel and Miss Etta Cone* (New York, 1962), 228.

156.   Edward Cone, "The Miss Etta Cones, the Steins, and M'sieu Matisse," *The American Scholar* 42 (1973), 454–455. My thanks to John Cauman for calling this article to my attention.

157.   Matisse to Simon Bussy, Hôtel des Thermes, Vittel, (25) August 1933. Shortly before Matisse left for Merion in May, he had written to his wife to look after the first version of the mural and make sure that the pinned pieces of paper did not fall off (Matisse to Amélie Matisse, 5 May 1933, Matisse Archives).

158.   Matisse to Pierre Matisse, 11 October 1933, Pierre Matisse Archives. A photograph of the mural that appears to have been taken in October 1933 is published in *Cahiers d'art* 10 (1–4) (1935), 10 (third from top).

159.   Matisse to Simon Bussy, 16 October 1933.

160.   This is clear from letters to Simon Bussy written on 5 November 1933 and 22 November 1933.

161.   Matisse to Pierre Matisse, 11 December 1933, Pierre Matisse Archives.

162.   Exchange of letters between Pierre Matisse and Matisse, 8 February 1934, Pierre Matisse Archives.

163.   Matisse to Pierre Matisse, 28 March 1934, Pierre Matisse Archives.

164.   Delectorskaya interview, 12 June 1992.

165.   Matisse wrote about this transaction in a letter to Simon Bussy, 31 July 1936. In this letter Matisse refers to the mural as "ma décoration des 'Nymphes' qui se trouve en 3 morceaux à Nice." He goes on to say that the panel would be hung high on the wall in the sculpture gallery and would be "presented with architectural vaults designed by the architect, a young man who is glad to have my work to show." He comments that originally Escholier had wanted to place the mural near the entrance, but that this was impossible because of the curved wall, "and it is impossible to dig into the surface that I worked so hard to keep planar." A few months later, on 10 November 1936, Matisse made a gift to the Musée du Petit Palais, Paris, of Cézanne's *Three Bathers,* which he had owned since 1899 (see Flam 1973, 75). On 22 January 1937, Matisse wrote to Escholier saying that he had been informed by the minister of commerce and industry that by decree of the commissioner-general of the 1937 exposition, "le panneau 'Les Nymphes'" had been acquired for the city of Paris (Musée d'art moderne de la Ville de Paris Archives). Although the two transactions were not officially related, the purchase of the mural may well have been a factor in Matisse's decision to give the museum his Cézanne.

166.   The purchase price was 95,000 francs (Musée d'art moderne de la Ville de Paris Archives).

167. While the mural was assigned to storage it was shown at several temporary exhibitions: in 1949 at the Palais des Papes in Avignon; in 1961 in the exhibition of Matisse's cutouts at the Musée des Arts Décoratifs, Paris; and in retrospective exhibitions in London (1968), Paris (1970), and Zurich (1982–1983).

168. So essential is this painting to Matisse's development that it has even been called the basis of the "Matisse System," by Yve-Alain Bois, "Matisse and 'Arche-drawing'," in *Painting as Model* (Cambridge, 1991), 3–63.

169. Maria Luz, "Témoignage: Henri Matisse," *XXe siècle,* n.s. 2 (January 1952), 55; trans. Flam 1973, 136. The interview took place in 1951.

170. Diehl 1946; trans. Flam 1973, 173.

171. In this version the sex of some of the figures is not entirely clear.

172. Joan Acocella, "Vaslav Nijinsky," in Nancy Van Norman Baer, *The Art of Enchantment: Diaghilev's Ballets Russes, 1909–1929* [exh. cat., Fine Arts Museum of San Francisco] (New York, 1988), 105.

173. Acocella 1988, 106–107. The quotations cited within this quotation are from Jacques Rivière's review of the ballet in *La nouvelle revue française* 10 (59) (1 November 1913).

174. E. Tériade, "Edouard Manet vu par Henri Matisse," *L'Intransigeant,* 25 January 1932, 5; as cited in Schneider 1984, 306 n.25 (retranslated here from the original French). The interview was given on the occasion of the large 1932 Manet retrospective.

175. Dudley 1934, 299–300.

176. Matisse to Pierre Matisse, 11 October 1933, Pierre Matisse Archives.

177. Matisse to Alexandre Romm, 19 January 1934; trans. Flam 1973, 68.

178. Romm to Matisse, 3 February 1934; Matisse to Romm, 14 February 1934; trans. Flam 1973, 68.

179. Matisse to Romm, 14 February 1934; trans. Flam 1973, 68–69.

180. Matisse to Romm, 14 February 1934; trans. Flam 1973, 69.

181. O'Brian 1991, 131.

182. Matisse to Romm, 14 February 1934; trans. Flam 1973, 69.

183. Schneider 1984, 616.

184. See Schneider 1984, 302.

185. Louis Aragon, "Matisse-en-France," in *Henri Matisse: Thèmes et variations* (Paris, 1943). The interview took place in 1942.

186. A few years before, Barnes had corresponded with Paul Guillaume about *Bathers by a River,* which Guillaume had recently purchased and was trying to sell, along with *The Piano Lesson,* now in the Museum of Modern Art, New York. In a letter of 6 October 1926, Barnes tacitly declined to buy the paintings and wrote Guillaume that as the *Bathers* was "the largest Matisse I ever heard of [it] should go into a public museum" (Barnes Foundation Archives).

187. Delectorskaya interview, 12 June 1992.

188. For a fascinating collection of in-progress photographs and relevant drawings, see Delectorskaya 1986 (English translation 1988). According to Lydia Delectorskaya, the mural panels were photographed when Matisse felt that he had brought them to a decisive stage in their evolution (Delectorskaya interview, 12 June 1992).

189. See the illustrations in Delectorskaya 1986, 58–67.

190. Matisse to Pierre Matisse, 11 July 1935, Pierre Matisse Archives.

191. E. Tériade, "Constance du fauvisme," *Minotaure* 2(11) (15 October 1936), 3.

Typeset in Monotype Dante, a typeface designed by Giovanni Mardersteig. Color separations are by Color Masters, Alexandria, Virginia. The book is printed on Potlatch Quintessence by Stephenson Printing, Alexandria, Virginia, and bound by American Trade Bindery, Baltimore, Maryland.